A GUIDE TO
BUSINESS
RESEARCH

A GUIDE TO
BUSINESS
RESEARCH

Developing, Conducting, and
Writing Research Projects

CHARLES B. SMITH

SECOND EDITION

Nelson-Hall Publishers/Chicago

Project Editor: Dorothy Anderson
Designer: Tamra Campbell-Phelps

Library of Congress Cataloging-in-Publication Data

Smith, Charles B.
    A guide to business research : developing, conducting, and writing
research projects / Charles B. Smith. — 2nd ed.
        p.   cm.
    Includes index.
    ISBN 0-8304-1229-8
    1. Business writing—Handbooks, manuals, etc.   2. Business—
Research—Methodology—Handbooks, manuals, etc.   I. Title.
HF5718.3.S65   1991
330'.072—dc20   90-47174
                                                                                CIP

Manufactured in the United States of America

10 9 8 7 6 5 4 3 2

Contents

Preface

As it was for the first edition of *A Guide to Business Research*, the purpose of this revised edition is to help business students with their research projects, theses, or dissertations. The intent is to provide a simple, straightforward *guide* for handling those elements in research that students say are the most perplexing or troublesome to them.

In response to users' comments and suggestions about the first edition, a chapter on scholarly writing practices and a list of 258 potential research projects have been added. Plus, additions to the original chapters have been made. As before, however, this revised edition is intended for undergraduate and graduate research and report writing.

This book differs from the conventional research methods text in the proportion of the type of material presented. That is, about half of the material in this book relates to the written presentation and half to research methods. Typically, one sees a research methods text with only one chapter or a portion of a chapter devoted to the written presentation. Yet, if researchers cannot present in a logical, orderly fashion what they did and what they found, they will have failed. The reader should not have to contend with an awkward or illogical presentation.

No pretense is made here for a full-fledged textbook on research methods and design. Many specialized texts in this area are available; therefore, the intent here is to provide an informal and practical approach to research as a *process.*

Materials and ideas in this book came from twenty-nine years of teaching, reading, and discussing ideas about research and writing. For the helpful comments and searching questions from hundreds of graduate students over the years, I owe a debt of appreciation. If I have taught them and helped them in their careers, I am grateful; they can be sure they have helped me to understand their needs in facilitating completion of a research project.

I have found the students want to know how to structure a research project—from scratch—and then how to present it in an acceptable manner. And they have found the bachelor's degree provides no magical transfer of training in report-writing ability to the graduate student. Therefore, if the students who use this book learn to appreciate a creditable research project and to not fear tackling such a project, then I shall have achieved my purpose.

1

Characterizing Research

Research is characterized by a wide range of meanings and activities. Some people may think of research in terms of a well-equipped laboratory, bustling scientists, and a formula-laden chalkboard. Others may think of research in terms of their own activities—that of casually reviewing newspapers, magazines, and journals, or asking a few questions when convenient, or using some trial-and-error methods. These are the people who are likely to comment, "I've done a little research on that."

Students may think of research in terms of reviewing indexes and copying information from various sources on note cards. When they assemble the data from these note cards, replete with footnotes containing a liberal sprinkling of ibid.'s and op. cit.'s, they say they have completed a "research" project.

Students working on an advanced degree, however, usually are required to show proficiency in scientific research procedures and presentation of the results. They probably view research as a graduate-student ritual. Slight wonder, since research probably appears to be the major hurdle to a graduate student's achieving an advanced degree. Too, beginning graduate students find the baccalaureate degree has conferred on them no magical transfer of training in research methods.

One has only to observe a typical student embarking on a research project, thesis, or dissertation. Very likely, the budding researcher ends up in the library reviewing completed theses and dissertations to imitate their organization and style. The trouble is, all these authors, too, have imitated their predecessors, and so on. The result is a perpetuation of a sterile, stereotyped, and sometimes illogical presentation; ignorance is compounded. The old saying is: "if you steal from one author, it's plagiarism. If you steal from many authors, it's research."

The spectrum of meanings of research, then, ranges from that of guesses or hunches based on a smattering of information collected haphazardly to that of conclusions reached by using scientific or systematic research methods. Thus, the purpose of this chapter is to examine the characteristics of the research process by:

1. Defining research
2. Determining the nature of creditable research
3. Reviewing the scientific method
4. Classifying research methods
5. Identifying the goals of research
6. Relating research to scholarship

Defining Research

You would probably find as many definitions of research as you would the number of authors writing about it. A review of these definitions shows most have the following elements or terms in common:

Activity	What Kind	Why
	systematic	to discover facts
inquiry	studious	to revise accepted princi-
investigation	critical	ples or conclusions
experimentation	diligent	to find new truths
examination	exhaustive	to avoid *status quo*
creation	orderly	
	objective	
	logical	

Research is an activity, a process, or a method; and two of the preceding lists are "what" and "why" qualifiers of the activity. You can see, then, that combinations of these words will serve to define research as is evident from definitions of research in other published works. For example, a selection of words from the foregoing lists can result in combinations such as these:
Research is:

- a systematic, studious inquiry to discover facts, to find new truths, and to avoid the *status quo*. (or)
- an orderly, exhaustive investigation to revise accepted principles or conclusions. (or)
- a diligent, objective examination to find new truths and revise accepted principles or conclusions.

The point is that you really can take your choice of definitions, provided you use the generally accepted terms as listed here.

But can't we have a better definition? Perhaps. Really, one important element in research is that of curiosity. Research requires of a person an attutide of inquisitiveness, that of "I wonder how . . ." or "I wonder why . . ." or "I wonder what. . . ." The researcher seeks to know reasons and causes behind events and behavior. So, now we can say: RESEARCH IS AN ACTIVITY CHARACTERIZED BY INTELLECTUAL CURIOSITY, USING SYSTEMATIC PLANNING TO COLLECT FACTS, PERFORMING OBJECTIVE ANALYSIS THROUGH LOGICAL THINKING, AND ENDING WITH A NEW TRUTH OR VERIFICATION OF AN EXISTING ONE.

Yet, with all the definitions of research available, apparently something more is needed. The wide ranges in quality evident in completed research projects, theses, and dissertations suggest criteria need to be established for creditable research.

Determining the Nature of Creditable Research

Creditable research means praiseworthy research; it measures up to today's accepted standards. One could ask these questions to determine creditability. When is research really research? Does the typical college term paper qualify as research? Does the market survey qualify as research? Does simulation or model building qualify as research? Does a history qualify as research? How do these types of projects compare with typical theses or dissertations? Are all of these types creditable research? More than likely, we would find that the depth of meaning of the word *research* varies with the person or group, even though the activity or process completed actually meets the broad definition of research given here.

Then, what characteristics make research creditable? Although the list of characteristics could be long, detailed, and subject to many people's whims, basically, five comprehensive characteristics are inherent in creditable research.

1. *A meaningful, limited, clearly defined problem.* Since the problem is the very basis of the research, it must have creditable characteristics of its own. (These characteristics are described in the next chapter.) The problem must be relatively significant, feasible, and clearly stated, preferably as a question requiring an answer. The problem must be limited or confined. You can hardly write about the world and all that is in it. The problem should be within your capabilities to handle. You should possess or have the ability to obtain the necessary background that will qualify you to undertake the research.

The commendable problem also opens the door for new problems and fields of investigation; it fosters curiosity that may, in the future, contribute to knowledge in general.

2. *A need or a purpose.* To satisfy an academic requirement is not enough of a purpose. Neither is an accidental finding made when you are not engaged in research a satisfactory need. A purpose or need should involve personal curiosity—a desire to solve a universal problem, to contribute to general knowledge, to change the *status quo,* to improve a situation. It should be in a field that offers promise for research and problems that need to be solved. A selfish purpose, the purpose confined to individual gain only, is excluded.

3. *An appropriate research design.* The research design must include consideration for all facets or aspects of the problem. The research cannot be classified as creditable if the methods used do not permit an appropriate, full, and detailed investigation. Creditable research usually employs the scientific method; that is, it follows a systematic plan, beginning with a problem statement and progressing through the stages of hypothesis statement (stated or implied), careful collection of facts, classification and analysis of facts, and generalizations from the facts. Although the problem may be worthy, inappropriate methods may render the research worthless.

4. *Proper collection and treatment of the data.* Creditable research must have a logical approach to the collecting and handling of research data. The techniques and procedures should relate only to answering the problem; extraneous data should be excluded. Authoritative, objective data should be preferred in place of biased, subjective data. Quantitative data, as well as qualitative data, should be gathered. Facts and conclusions accumulated by other investigators should be part of the raw material.

Facts are not worth much alone; they achieve value only through analysis and interpretation leading to properly supported, clear, decisive conclusions. Without such properly supported conclusions, the research will not be creditable no matter how extensive the investigation. It must end in new truths for any reader, not opinions slanted to satisfy a particular group or to prove a point.

5. *A complete, logical, and orderly presentation.* The mechanics of presentation should be appropriate to the problem

and conform to accepted research presentations. If a problem has been fully investigated and logical conclusions drawn, the proper presentation of the information will help to determine the research creditability. Regardless of how valid and acceptable the research may be, you can hide your efforts completely through an inept, inaccurate, illogical presentation. Unfortunately, the converse is not true. An exceptional presentation will not salvage a poor job in research. Creditable research leads a reader through the problem and its solution with ease, while satisfying any anticipated curiosity of the reader in the process. The material is properly organized, classified, and coordinated in the research presentation. Good format and writing style help put across the research to the reader.

Creditable research, then, must have a meaningful problem, be purposeful, employ appropriate procedures, have properly supported conclusions stemming from logical analyses, be presented in proper form, and be based upon the scientific method.

Reviewing the Scientific Method

The term *scientific method* is somewhat a misnomer—it's not really a method in the sense of a formal procedure. Rather, it is a rigorous, systematic approach to problem solving that has evolved from the work of pioneers in science. Research for problem solving in most disciplines has followed three previous approaches: trial and error; authority and tradition; and speculation and argumentation (philosophizing).

The scientific method is the offspring of a branch of philosophy called *epistemology* (from the Greek *episteme*—for knowledge, and *logos*—for theory). In the seventeenth century, Francis Bacon attempted to provide a blueprint for acquisition of "scientific knowledge." He offered a fourfold rule of work: observe, measure, explain, and then verify. By the nineteenth century, a more sophisticated version was offered:

- pose a question about nature
- collect pertinent evidence

- form an explanatory hypothesis
- derive its implications
- test them experimentally
- accept, reject, or modify the hypothesis accordingly.

The scientific method is based upon the assumption that events in nature have a cause and a natural explanation and are repeatable. It involves following certain "rules" as evolved from the work of pioneers in science, so that the knowledge obtained in the investigation will be more reliable than that obtained by a "seat-of-the-pants" approach or a trial-and-error method. Thus, the scientific method relates to how reliable knowledge is obtained. In fact, the method can be viewed as an attitude or a philosophy that provides guidance for researchers. So, although not all research may have scientific results or conclusions, all creditable research does use scientific procedures—the scientific method.

The scientific method itself has been the subject of many books, some with diverse views about the method. These writings reflect variations in the number of steps in the scientific method, but these variations stem only from the method the various authors use to classify the steps. As viewed here, the following are the logical steps in the research process using the scientific method:

1. *Select a field, topic, or subject,* preferably related to your expertise and interest

2. *Select a problem*

through:	your curiosity
	your experience
	asking authorities
	updating research
evaluate by asking:	Is it feasible?
	Are data available?
	Are methods available?
	Is it interesting?
	Will it make a contribution?
limit by:	dividing
	asking questions

                factoring
                reducing variables
                restricting scope

3. *Construct a preliminary bibliography*
    by using: indexes
                      card catalogs
                      bibliographies

4. *Develop a research design*
    by: reviewing literature and research
                      constructing hypotheses
                      developing research procedures
                      determining data analysis
                          approach

5. *Make a research proposal*
    by stating: tentative title
                      problem background
                      the research problem
                      the research objective and need
                      the study scope and limitations
                      definitions of terms
                      the research design
                      tentative project outline
                      the working bibliography

6. *Collect data*
    through: secondary sources
                      primary sources (or both)
                      by experiment
                      by survey (interviews,
                        questionnaires, observation)

7. *Organize data*
    by: classifying data
                      testing the outline
                      formulating preliminary tables
                        and graphics

8. *Analyze data*
    by: testing hypotheses
                      noting trends, relationships,

                  implications, causes, effects,
                  significance, comparisons,
                  contrasts

9. *Derive conclusions*
   to: answer the research problem
                  note significance of findings
                  point out implications

10. *Write the research report*
   by: making a scholarly presentation
                  publishing the results
                  integrating the findings in the
                     literature

The foregoing list is somewhat arbitrary both in the order of presentation and in the number of steps listed. For example, one researcher may determine the elements of the problem before surveying the field of literature. Perhaps the steps could be reduced to nine by combining steps four and five. What is important is that, regardless of the order of the steps or the number of steps, all of the elements of the scientific method have been included when the research is completed.

The development of scientific methods of investigations has led the way to more efficient research. The importance of research method cannot be overestimated in the advances that have been made as a result of scientific research carried out in all disciplines.

Identifying the Goals of Research

Traditionally, research has been classified by the researcher's goal or purpose for undertaking research—that of *pure* or *applied* research.

Pure research is also known as *basic, fundamental, disinterested,* or *free.* Pure research is characterized as having no prevailing goal and of being of interest only to one's colleagues. The major thrust is a deeper understanding of the universe and the phenomena within it. Completed pure research may lead to the question: "Of what use is it?" Such a question no doubt was asked about the discovery of X-rays and the laser. The National Science Foundation classifies basic research as an activity directed toward increase of knowledge in science with the primary aim of the investigator having a fuller knowledge or understanding of the subject under study rather than for a practical application. *Applied* research is also known as *practical* or *action oriented*; the primary value is to an employer or to the public. Overall, the results of research are what count regardless of whether the impetus was basic or applied.

The distinction is very difficult to make in the behavioral and social sciences; applied research is done to uncover practical ways of using the findings from pure research. Hindsight can produce a dividing line between basic and applied research; that is, did the research produce new knowledge, new facts, or a new understanding? If so, it was basic. A fact often acknowledged is that one person's basic research is another person's applied research.

Sometimes the distinction between basic and applied research may be a matter of time. In the 1950s, symbolic logic was the purest branch of mathematics. Today it is heavily applied, as in computers. A comment heard a few years ago was that "the laser was a solution in search of a problem." Then, when holograms were produced, someone said, "We now have a use for the laser—to make holograms. Now we need to find an application for holograms." Even though the distinction between the two goals is sometimes hazy, however, intellectual curiosity or scholarship is basic to the goal, wherever it may lie on the classification continuum.

The Student and Research

Business literature supports the idea that knowledge about research methods is useful for students preparing for careers in management because:

1. Knowledge about the organization has grown at a phenomenal rate in recent years. If managers are to be so-

phisticated consumers of this information, they need to understand the process that generates such information.

2. Students need the ability to evaluate the quality of research. Skepticism toward research is preferred to indiscriminate acceptance of findings.
3. The problems researchers and managers face are similar; that is, identify the problem, construct hypotheses (managers may use hunches), and conduct a systematic data collection.

Too often, students don't appreciate one of the real purposes for doing a research study and writing the report—to think systematically and to write clearly. Many have not been forced to express themselves clearly and concisely. It's not until they begin their research report that the deficiency is noted.

Most undergraduate work is aimed at broadening and diversifying the educational growth of a person. Programs stress a "liberalizing function." Thus, the undergraduate term paper emphasis is on learning in a field and reviewing facts already known.

Graduate work gives intensive study in a special field. Students are encouraged to work independently and to develop their own plan of study and research. Their research attempts to discover new truths, which demands a critical attitude. Graduate students must become familiar with the existing body of knowledge and recognize that the world is littered with half truths and some absolute untruths. Too, the master's degree emphasis is on developing research competence with less concern for the significance of the findings. Doctoral research, however, is expected to contribute to knowledge—to develop new facts, theories, or principles. For all college students, then, research should reflect a level of scholarship expected of people holding a college degree.

Relating Research to Scholarship

Scholarship may be defined as learning or knowledge acquired by study, or academic attainments of a scholar. A *scholar* is a learned person who has a profound knowledge of a subject. The term also connotes analytical thought processes coupled with correctness of self-expression. These definitions become significant when they are related to the research process involving diligent inquiry or investigation into a subject for the purpose of discovering facts, theories, or applications.

Scholarship and research, therefore, are similar in their definitions. From these ideas, one may say that scholarly research is meaningful to others as well as to the researcher; it involves original thinking; it conforms to accepted methods; it is adequate in complexity and depth; its language is clear, coherent, logical, and grammatically correct; and it is an orderly presentation with an appropriate style and format.

With the characteristics of research set out in this chapter, the next chapter contains a description of the selection and development of the research problem.

2

Selecting and Developing the Research Problem

Perhaps the most important step in the research process is selecting and developing the problem for research. Developing the problem sometimes is more important than its solution, which may just require mathematical or experimental ability. A familiar saying is, "A problem well stated is a problem half solved." Many students, sometimes far along in their research, find that their research problems are too large, or indefinite, or trivial, or not really researchable. These and many other hazards are likely to stem from a poorly selected and stated problem.

The quality of the problem statement is crucial—and it involves more than the researcher. In the complex activities of today, it's also a question for the teacher of research, the supervising professor of a thesis or dissertation, a company research director, and those who administer the research funds. Selecting a problem, then, requires creative imagination to raise new questions or possibilities and to regard old questions from a new perspective.

Selecting a Problem

Beginners in research often have difficulty selecting a research problem because of their lack of familiarity in a field and what has been accomplished in it. For them, it is often a formidable task, one that requires a great deal of creativity. Failure to define a framework of inquiry invites—even guarantees—enormous waste. A researcher may fail to identify a problem accurately because:

1. The researcher doesn't perceive the problem or doesn't define it correctly. This dilemma can stem from a problem too complex for comprehension, a closed mind, or a lack of experience in the area.
2. The researcher sees the wrong problem or wrong causes, or both. The situation may be a mix of several problems interwoven; the situation may be a symptom of a more complex problem, or a wrong inference may be made.
3. The researcher may think that doing *something* is better than doing *nothing;* the problem-identification phase is ignored.

A problem suitable for graduate-level research generally requires a persistent search on the part of the student. Seldom does a student enter a graduate program with an acceptable research problem already in hand. Too, members of the student's graduate committee usually frown on furnishing the student with a research problem. The student's selecting and answering a research problem help to provide evidence of the person's intellectual maturity.

Following are leads to help in the selection of a problem:

1. Look for suggestions in periodical articles in your major field of interest. Articles sometimes report studies that may point out aspects needing further investigation.

2. Question the validity of a generally accepted practice in some field of endeavor.
3. Look for holes or gaps in explanations or in accepted principles. Note practices at variance with theory.
4. Talk with authorities in your field of interest, with faculty, with businessmen, with government agency employees, and with union officials.
5. Examine completed studies for possible recommendations for further research. Review *Dissertation Abstracts* for possible leads to a problem.
6. Note what studies need redoing after a reasonable time span; update research.
7. Make a contribution by synthesizing and analyzing research, or literature, or both in a particular field.
8. Record and analyze an occurrence, a phenomenon, or an entity for an historical study.
9. Redo a study to add to its credence or to check its accuracy. Or, if done in one segment of industry or geographical area, compare it with another.
10. Evaluate the effectiveness of a certain practice or determine an acceptable procedure from alternatives.
11. Develop new ideas or models to analyze a controversial area.
12. Be alert for issues brought out in class discussions or lectures.
13. Look for likenesses and differences in a field; see points of controversy; note deficiencies in explanations.
14. Determine how one segment of an industry compares with that in another industry.
15. Look for interdisciplinary relationships; explore how one discipline is related to another.
16. Look for areas where knowledge or information is scarce, out of date, or indefinite.
17. Identify current thought on a subject or resolve current problems and issues in a subject or field.

Appendix D contains additional potential areas or situations for research. With the foregoing suggestions serving as potential leads to selection of a problem, you need to evaluate the quality of your research problem as you finally select it.

Evaluating the Problem

If your research is at the graduate level, your graduate committee usually has final approval of the research problem. The following criteria will help you evaluate the quality of your research problem.

Scholarly acceptability. The problem is:
- original to the extent it will make a contribution to knowledge.
- concrete and explicit; in question form; subproblems are listed.
- the next logical problem in the field to answer.
- exclusive; no one has a prior claim to it.
- of interest to the general public of scholars and practitioners; interest is not confined to the researcher alone or to one institution.

Depth and complexity. The problem:
- is narrow, but not so narrow as to be trivial or insignificant.
- may be expanded into other fields.
- will answer a practical and immediate need when answered; significant for the field; timely.
- expresses a relationship between two or more variables.
- provides a basis for analysis, not mere fact grubbing.

Researchability. The problem is one for which:
- adequate data are available; cooperation can be obtained from those people who must participate.
- adequate techniques or instruments or both are available.
- data can be treated objectively; not dependent only upon value judgments.
- research will not be too costly in time or money.
- the possibility of empirical testing is present.

Researcher accountability. For you, as the researcher, the problem:
- is one for which you have the requisite skills or can obtain them.

- is one in which you have a personal interest.
- is closely related to your field of concentration.
- will provide experiences to stimulate your intellectual growth.

In addition to the foregoing criteria for problem evaluation, you must know the body of research and techniques related to a problem area. Sometimes naivete is a source of joy, but it's not so in creditable research efforts. You should be able to disbelieve, to be dissatisfied with, or to deny knowledge or beliefs you now have. Valued research seems to stem from dissatisfaction with the way things are, rather than agreeable perpetuation of present ways of doing things. You need to see the forest beyond the trees and test the generality of your proposed results. We cannot be geniuses, but at least we can try to be less trivial. We can learn as much as we can and believe in new ways.

A research problem very likely will not meet all the criteria just listed; but since problem evaluation often is made by graduate committees or supervising professors, the list does provide a basis for determining how well the problem selected meets the frequently used criteria. The next step is to state the problem.

Stating the Problem

One of the most important steps in the research process consists of *clearly* stating the research problem. This step includes selecting a manageable portion of an area or topic for study. As mentioned previously, ". . . a problem well put is a problem half solved." A problem well put is in the form of a question raised for an answer.

Sometimes the problem is referred to as the *topic* or the *purpose*. These terms, however, are imprecise for use here and may distract you from your real or intended problem. A *topic* is really a subject for discussion. If a problem is cloaked in terms of a topic, the vagueness may lead to the collection of much useless data that do not contribute to an answer to the problem. The same is true for *purpose*. Purpose connotes an aim or objective—a "why" for tackling the research. And, research cannot have a purpose; only *you* can. A *problem*, however, is the "what" of research. Thus, casting the problem in the form of a question leads to precision by helping you to:

- establish boundaries to the research (you can't write about the world and all that's in it).
- construct hypotheses.
- build a research design.
- organize the written presentation.
- be precise in formulating the answer to the problem.

Topic or purpose constructions do not offer these advantages. As a help in stating a problem, you may start your thinking with "I wonder. . . ." For example:

I wonder whether the number of days needed for work sampling studies can be reduced.

I wonder what guidelines are needed for management to convert to a management information system.

I wonder what the current effects of the legal environment are on advertising.

I wonder what impact coupon fraud and misredemption has on the manufacturer, the retailer, and the consumer.

With the problem statement in the form of a tentative question, observe the following guides:

1. Phrase the question in a form that will elicit more than a mere *yes* or *no* answer; provide for a range in the answer.

   NOT: "Do published financial statements provide relevant and adequate information to meet the needs of present and future stockholders?" (A simple yes or no would answer this question.)

BUT: "To what extent do published financial state-
        ments provide. . .?" (This question can't be an-
        swered yes or no; a range is needed.)
NOT: "Are there any trends in the incidence or pattern
        of price leadership from 1950 to 1985?" (Again,
        simply yes or no would answer the question.)
BUT: "What have been the trends in the incidence or
        pattern of price leadership . . .?"

2. Avoid phrasing value-judgement types of questions.
Such questions aren't researchable—they have no answer. A value judgment is an estimate of the goodness or
worth of a person, action, or event, especially when
such an estimate is not called for or desired. Especially,
a judgment is an expression of a person's approval or dis-
approval of something. A frailty of such a question is
that the researcher tends to ignore negative data—data
that do not support the desired answer. Value-judgment
questions are usually prefaced with "should . . . ?"

NOT: "Should the Federal Government adopt a compre-
        hensive program to control land use in the United
        States?"
BUT: "What are the implications and the current
        thought on the federal government adopting a pro-
        gram to control land use in the United States?"
NOT: Should nuclear energy be banned?

        Should advertising be banned from children's
        television programs?

        Should abortions be legalized?

        Do managers need a code of ethics?

        Is sex in advertising affecting the moral charac-
        ter of Americans?

Answers to the foregoing questions will result in position papers—not creditable research.

3. If possible, phrase the question in *analytic* form, one
   that deals with *cause-and-effect* relationship. It is an *if-*

then approach. Such phrasing forces precision and furnishes a better basis for generalization in analysis.

NOT: "Has the practice of price leadership had an effect on social and legal attitudes toward concentration of market power?"

BUT: "What effect has the practice of price leadership had on social and legal attitudes toward concentration of market power?"

OR: "If one advertises on the radio, in newspapers, and in magazines, which medium will be most effective in persuading consumers to buy brand items?"

In contrast to the analytic question, a *descriptive-form* question only identifies and analyzes a situation—it's a *status-quo* approach. For example:

"What is the nature of managerial succession practices of selected small electronics manufacturing companies in the Phoenix, Arizona, metropolitan area?"

or

"What is the current thought on variable-rate residential mortgages?"

But note that some descriptive questions suggest a mere listing of factors as an answer, with no need for analysis:

"What factors have recently accounted for the changing competitive framework of the beer industry?"

or

"What qualities make an effective personnel manager?"

To recap, an analytical question is likely to provide a more important contribution than is a descriptive question. Descriptive-type questions are concerned only with identification or status-quo situations, whereas analytical questions reflect cause-effect or if-then relationships.

The analytical question involves variables; and as the number of variables increases, so does the complexity of the problem. The following are examples of analytical problems showing how increasing numbers of variables are structured on the basis of abstract representations.

1. "What are the effects of Japanese import competition on the consumer electronics industry?"

2. "What are the effects of American work ethics (A), work standards (B), and customs (C) on foreign employees (D)?"

3. "What are the effects of repair costs (A), legal procedures (B), and auto thefts (C) on the insurance companies (D) and the auto owners (E)?"

4. "What has been the impact of three alternate work schedules: staggered work hours (A), shortened work week (B), and flexitime (C) on selected factors from the standpoint of problems and benefits for the City of Phoenix (D), City employees (E), and the community (F)?"

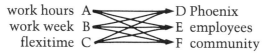

Factoring the Research Problem

Factoring a research problem involves identifying subquestions that stem from the overall general question. The sub-

questions, when answered, provide in total the answer to the
overall problem. Factoring, like outlining, is a process of division and addition.

Note that you cannot have only one subquestion. You
can't divide something and end up with only one part. If you
see what you believe is the only subquestion, you have a *twofold* problem. Say, "The problem for this research is twofold"
and then list your *two* questions. Also, be aware that you can
overlist subquestions to a problem. Should you end up with,
perhaps, more than four subquestions, then more grouping is
needed to reduce the list. Too many subquestions will cause a
problem in organizing the outline.

The factoring process includes considering the problem *scope* as a restricting device. Otherwise, as one often
hears, the attempt is made to write about the world and all
that's in it. You can generally confine the problem question
in terms of

- time
- place (geographic)
- types (characteristics, factors, criteria, variables)
- quantities
- combinations of the foregoing

Further, the factoring process may generate hypotheses for
testing when the problem is stated analytically. These processes are shown graphically in Figures 2.1 and 2.2.

Developing Hypotheses

An hypothesis is a tentative answer to the research problem;
it is a proposition that can be tested statistically or with empirical data and rules of logic. Your task is to collect data to
test the validity of the hypothesis. You cannot avoid hypothesis formulation because it goes on in your mind whether or
not you state it explicitly. Sometimes you may not even be
aware of it. Any researcher would have assumptions about
what might be found, and these assumptions form the basis

for an hypothesis. An hypothesis, then, is built on assumptions, and the hypothesis carries the idea of testing for ultimate validation: assumptions do not.

An explicit hypothesis helps to guide the investigation. It establishes boundaries, it narrows the research, it helps you to organize your thinking, and it conditions and improves the design of tests. Most research questions and hypotheses can be alternate forms of each other because a question is implicit in the hypothesis. Yet, not all questions can be *stated* in the form of an hypothesis. Such would be true of the question that requires only description of a situation; that is, fact finding and analysis. Thus, not all research projects necessarily will have hypotheses. Because some hypotheses are difficult to test in the social sciences, sometimes the step is simply omitted from the scientific method. Some types of research may very well have a "working or tentative hypothesis" for use only in guiding the investigation. The completed research has no mention of the hypothesis since no validation of an hypothesis took place. For example, philosophical research, prognostic research, case study research, and some descriptive research may have no hypothesis validation.

Two types of hypotheses generally recognized are the *research hypothesis* and the *statistical* or *null hypothesis.* The *research hypothesis* cannot be analyzed statistically; it is an explanatory hypothesis constructed to serve as a guide in developing the research design. Usually it is in the form of an assertion containing a prediction based upon certain conditions. This assertion may be in the previously mentioned "if . . . then" format; for example, "If the brand item is advertised via TV, the radio, and direct mail, then TV will be the most effective in getting people to buy the item."

For the example of factoring questions using Camper's World, given in Figure 2.1, the research hypothesis would be:

1. Savings in freight, duties, labor, and materials will result in a substantial, overall product cost saving.
2. The cost saving will facilitate a competitive consumer price in the European market.

3. The competitive prices will generate increased sales. (Prognostic: not a testable hypothesis for completion of the study.)
4. Increased European sales will return a suitable level of profit to Camper's World.

Or, the research hypothesis may be simply: "Phoenix hospitals' overall experience with wage incentive systems has

FIGURE 2.1

Factoring the Research Problem

1. *Research Topic*	Expansion of Camper's World production facilities to Europe.
2. *Research Problem*	Cast the research topic (1) into a question—*descriptive* or *analytic.*
2a. *Descriptive Problem*	What are the implications of expanding Camper's World production facilities to Europe? Factor the foregoing descriptive problem into subquestions by asking questions *about* the problem; e.g., *what* implications from *what* standpoints?
or	
2b. *Analytical Problem*	What is the feasibility of establishing a Camper's World branch assembly plant in Europe? That is, will such a branch plant reduce product price to such a point that it will result in substantially increased sales?
3. *Your Premise*	IF: (a) savings in freight, duties, labor, and material will make possible a substantial overall product cost savings; and (b) this cost savings will facilitate a competitive consumer price in the European market; and

been unfavorable stemming from employee resistance to implementation and maintenance of the program."

The *null* or *statistical hypothesis* is statistical in nature because it is always stated in a manner to permit the calculation of the probability of each possible result. Aside from testing the probability of a possible result, the *degree* of relationship may be determined.

Following are examples of null hypotheses:

FIGURE 2.1 (Continued)

	(c) competitive prices will generate increased sales; and
	(d) the increased European sales will return a suitable level of profit to Camper's World
	THEN:
	(c) establishment of a Camper's World branch assembly plant in Europe is feasible.
4. *Subhypotheses*	Give your perceived answers to the foregoing—an evaluation of your beliefs concerning (a), (b), (c), and (d) as based upon your assumptions.
	THEREFORE:
5. *Hypothesis*	The European branch assembly plant is (or is not) feasible. Establish decision criteria for determining the basis for accepting or rejecting your hypothesis.
6. *Problem Subquestions*	Cast your *premise* statements into questions. Answers to each of these questions *must* contribute to answering your research problem. Also, each of these subquestions will likely yield a chapter or a major division in your completed project.

To determine both the validity and practicality of fewer sampling days (fewer than the work cycle of fifteen days) in a work
sample, the following hypothesis was developed: Fewer work-
sampling days provide an estimate that is not significantly different from the estimate of the original study which was developed with a greater number of days in the work sample.
        —Arthur Jacobs, Arizona State University

The hypothesis tested for each of the fifteen variables questioned, stated in null form, is that: No relationship exists at
the .05 significance level between the variable and time de-

FIGURE 2.2

Factoring the Research Problem

1. *Research Topic*	Current practices and developments in role playing as a means of developing human relations skills in management.
2. *Research Problem*	Cast the research topic (1) into a question—*descriptive* or *analytic*—or both to yield a twofold problem.
2a. *Descriptive Problem*	What are the current practices and developments in role playing in developing human relations skills among management trainees?
and	
2b. *Analytical Problem*	To what extent does the attitude of management trainees toward multiple role playing serve as a method of developing human relations skills?
3. *Your Premise*	IF:
	management trainees
	(a) are exposed to role playing situations; and
	(b) become involved in the exercise; and
	(c) can relate the exercise to their work experience
	THEN:

---

posit levels. That is, it is hypothesized that the degree of relationship between each of the variables and time deposits, as expressed by the partial correlation coefficient, is not significantly different from zero.

    —Harry Jones, Arizona State University

    The null hypothesis is one of "no difference between groups" or "no prejudice" formulated with the express purpose of being rejected. The analysis of variance and related statistical techniques are used for testing the null hypothesis.

FIGURE 2.2 (Continued)

	(d) their attitude toward multiple role playing will furnish a basis for developing human relations skills.
4. *Subhypotheses*	(a) the management trainee has been sufficiently exposed to role playing situations; and
	(b) he becomes involved in the exercise; and
	(c) he can relate the situation to his work experience.
	THEREFORE:
5. *Working Hypothesis*	The management trainee's attitude toward multiple role playing will furnish a basis for determining its applicability for developing human relations skills.
6. *Problem Subquestions*	1. To what extent has the management trainee been exposed to role playing situations?
	2. How does the trainee perceive his participation in the role playing situation?
	3. To what extent is the trainee able to relate the role playing situation to his work experience?

You must select the probability value that must be reached before you decide to reject the null hypothesis. Use of a .05 significance level as a criterion for hypothesis acceptance means that the results during the sample period could have occurred by chance no more than 5 percent of the time, provided that the sample is random. And, when you are accepting or rejecting a statistical hypothesis on the basis of a sample, two types of judgment errors may result. These are called Type 1 errors and Type 2 errors. In a Type 1 error, the null hypothesis is rejected when it should be accepted. In a Type 2 error, the null hypothesis is accepted when it should be rejected.

Normally, hypothesis testing procedures are inappropriate when dealing with *population* data (rather than a sample), because any relationships determined from the population are significant by definition, and no inferences need be made. The merits of hypotheses can be set out as:

1. Hypotheses should be restricted in scope to match the problem and subproblems.
2. Hypotheses should be stated in simple, understandable terms. Complexity doesn't make them significant.
3. Hypotheses should be testable. Sometimes hypotheses can't be tested because the variables can't be measured or because they are based on value judgments.
4. Hypotheses should state relationships between variables.

Finally, you should remember that you do not *prove* an hypothesis; such a word is too final. A better choice would connote a degree of acceptance with such words as *substantiate, validate, verify,* or *accept.*

As you are formulating the problem, you also are building a research design. As has been mentioned, the steps in the orderly research process are not carried out one at a time; rather, you work on several steps at the same time. While you are formulating your problem, you are also reviewing the literature and research and deciding on data sources and collection methods. Once the problem has been selected and defined, you are ready to develop a research design as is discussed in Chapter 3, next.

3
Building a Research Design

After the problem is formulated, you begin the development of the research strategy or design—a detailed plan of the research undertaking. You know *what* you will investigate; now you must decide *how* you will conduct the inquiry. Precision in mapping the research design pays dividends in time saved through avoiding false starts, wrong routes, and hazy approaches. As considered here, research *design* does not mean the same as research *method*. The method is only a part of the overall research design.

You must be sure your research design will provide a specific answer to your research question; you will do *no more* and *no less* than you promise in your problem statement as confined by the scope. All parts of your completed research project must add up to the whole—that which is asked in the research problem. Data included merely because it is interesting, nice to know, or because the "pearls" are difficult to discard simply cannot be justified in a research project. Such inclusion shows fuzzy thinking or a lack of direction, or both—perhaps as a result of a poor research design.

When we read published research, we're often more interested in the results section than in the less glamorous section describing how the results came about. We tend to lose sight of the fact that a researcher's most important work may take place before going into the field or analyzing data. If choices of problem and method are made wisely, the data collection and analysis are simply implementations of the previous decision. The sources of the largest errors in business research are nonstatistical. That is, they stem from the following:

1. not identifying the proper question to investigate.
2. not identifying the nature and boundaries of the particular study or population involved.
3. not finding valid, accurate yardsticks to measure the phenomenon being investigated and in being sure what aspects should be measured.
4. not developing a consistent, appropriate research design.

And, building a research design involves the following factors:

- continuing the review of literature and research.
- constructing hypotheses, if needed.
- deciding on data collection methods—survey, experiment, case, secondary data, and sampling considerations, if any. Sometimes the nature of the question itself dictates the method to be used.
- constructing instruments needed for data collection, e.g., questionnaires, interview guide, measuring scales, and tests.
- setting up a pilot study, if needed. A pilot study can be used to determine the validity and reliability of tests.
- deciding on data analysis techniques—decision criteria for accepting or rejecting hypotheses.
- developing and writing a research proposal.

As mentioned before, research usually involves the use of two or more methods. At this stage, you know whether the research basically is *descriptive, experimental, creative,* or combinations of these types.

Determining the Research Approach

The nature of the research problem, the factoring of the problem into subquestions, the hypotheses constructed (if any), and the review of literature determine for the most part the approach selected for conducting the research.

Descriptive Research

Descriptive research is fact finding with interpretation and analysis of trends in attitudes, events, and facts in terms of their commonality and potential for prediction. This type of research includes normative survey, genetic, case, activity analysis, and historical or documentary methods.

Experimental Research

Experimental research is the controlled observation of change and development in which only one circumstance is varied while all other circumstances are held constant. This research includes model building and simulation. It answers the "how" and "why."

Creative Research

Creative research involves an analysis of ideas and theories and the production of ideas or objects of aesthetic or cultural value to society. This type of research includes philosophical, critical analysis; theoretical, synthesis, or conceptual methods; and objective creation of art forms.

The important idea here, therefore, is not what particular methods are called, or even that they are given names, but rather that the researcher clearly understands and can describe the research procedures used in the research proposal.

Writing the Research Proposal

The research proposal is a structured presentation of what you plan to do in research and how you plan to do it. The proposal gives those concerned with your research venture an opportunity to evaluate your research approach. Since proposal formats vary among organizations and in schools, the approach here is to provide guidelines for both a business-use proposal and an academic-use proposal. The guides shown are possibilities only; the best approach for your proposal is to find out what is wanted and then structure the proposal to suit those who will review it.

Suggested Proposal Content for Business Use

1. Tentative title and date.
2. Research objectives; what you propose to do.
3. Researcher or research staff qualifications (if appropriate).
4. Nature of the problem:
   • if exploratory, say so.
   • questions you expect to answer.
   • hypotheses you plan to test.
   • difficulties expected.
   • definitions of terms or constructs.
5. Proposed approach:
   • information required and data sources.
   • general procedures, e.g., sampling plan, pilot test, statistical techniques for presenting and interpreting data.
6. Time and cost considerations, if appropriate. Include a budget if appropriate.
7. Expected results or findings.
8. Working bibliography.

Proposals submitted for research grants or for manufacturing contracts will vary in structure as set out by the agency involved; such types are likely to differ markedly from the format given here.

Suggested Proposal Content for Academic Use

1. Tentative title and date.
2. Background information; what gives rise to the problem.
3. Problem statement; show problem factoring.
4. Problem amenities:
   - hypotheses, if any.
   - purpose or need or both.
   - scope or limitations or both.
   - definitions of terms, if needed.
5. Review of related literature and research.
6. Proposed procedures:
   - general approach; data sources.
   - sampling plan; pilot test; statistical techniques for presenting and interpreting data.
7. Working outline.
8. Preliminary bibliography.

Students sometimes are required to include a proposal-approval page with their proposal. With advisor or faculty approval, this approval page may serve as a "research contract" between the student and the advisor or graduate committee. When you structure your proposal as described here, you will have nearly written the first chapter (sometimes the first two or three chapters) of your research report. Perhaps you will need to do little more than change tense in your presentation from future tense to present and past tense. Also, instructors are likely to prefer a proposal in the fifteen- to thirty-page category (or an abstract of a longer proposal). As with the business-use proposal, the foregoing elements are possibilities; your best approach is to find out what is wanted and then structure your proposal to suit those who will review it.

Describing Proposal Elements

With the academic proposal structure set out, the following section contains descriptions and suggestions for structuring the specific elements in the proposal.

Tentative Research Title

Use a reasonably short title—seventeen to twenty words maximum—that relates directly to your research problem. A variant form of your problem statement usually is close. Avoid including such superfluous words as "A study of . . ." and "An investigation of. . . ."

Statement of the Problem

Provide background information about the problem to orient the reader. This review provides a logical transition to the specific problem statement that follows. On the basis of what you have just said, a problem needs answering. Lead off by stating the specific problem you plan to investigate (preferably in question form) and list subquestions with any problem interpretation, if needed. Include in this section your hypotheses, if any, or set the hypotheses out in a section parallel to "Statement of the Problem" such as "Hypotheses to Be Tested." And, make sure your tentative title is consistent with your problem statement.

Purpose (or Objective)

Your purpose is the "why" for doing the study—its objective. If you include this section, be sure it is not a mere restatement of your problem.

Need for the Study

In this section you should point out why the study is significant, the implications your findings may have, and who needs the answers. This need section may also be combined with the purpose section, such as "Purpose and Need for the Study."

Scope

The scope consists of the boundaries you have established for the study. The scope may describe geographical boundaries, a segment of a universe, or a time period. In addition, you may want to tell why you are *not* covering some specific facets in your study.

Limitations

Tell here the limitations (handicaps) of time, money, availability of data, subjectiveness of data, and the like that are *imposed* on you. In no instance, however, should these limitations furnish an excuse for poor performance or the quality of your work. Be sure your reader can distinguish between your scope and limitations by using headings, key words, or paragraphing. The limitations section may be combined with the foregoing section, "Scope," depending upon how you want to present it.

Definitions of Terms

Although you may assume your reader has a working knowledge of your research area, you still need to be on solid ground by being sure you agree on nebulous terms. Get your readers in step with you by defining terms that may be new or subject to different meanings. The definitions you use should be stated in simple terms, arranged alphabetically, and grammatically consistent. You may define terms by using a dictionary, by citing an authority, by giving an example, by excluding, or by analogy. What, for example, do you mean by "manager," "working days," "discount house," "fireproof," "furniture," "unmarried," "older worker," or "executive"?

Related Literature and Research

Give a short digest, perhaps one page, of the closely related research studies you found. Describe the extent of the literature and research in the field. For the related work, be sure to include bibliographic data in terms of author, title, date, place, the problem, and results. Chapter 4 contains a more detailed description of the approach to related literature because it is a part of the documentary search as described in that chapter.

Procedures

Present an overview of your research design—how you will conduct your investigation. Describe your sources of data and methods of collection. Although for the research proposal the procedures section may be a subdivision, it may very well be a separate chapter in your final research report. Which you do depends upon the detail needed to describe the procedures. If the section on procedures would be out of proportion in the coordinate elements in the "Introduction," then a separate chapter should be used for describing them.

The basic criterion for describing procedures in the final research report should be completeness—so complete that your reader could repeat the study and come up with findings similar to yours. For the proposal, however, the detail need not be so complete. Yet, you do need to tell why you choose to do what you say here. Anticipate reader questions and objections and meet them with explanations and justifications.

Tell about the instruments, forms, models, resources, or statistical techniques you plan to use, any validity or reliability tests proposed. Tell how you plan to select your sample, whether you will use a pilot study, how interviews will be set up, and your planned means of evaluation and analysis. If you are doing secondary data collection only, then list the sources you will consult and describe the method of analysis.

Tentative General Outline

In outline form, reflect your preliminary thinking about how you plan to organize your material. The following sample topic outline will get you started:

I. Introduction
   (Background information)
   Statement of problem
   Purpose and need
   Scope and limitations
   Definitions of terms
   Research design
   Organizational plan

II. Review of Related Literature and Research
III. Procedures
IV. ⎫
V. ⎬ (content chapters—
VI. ⎭ use tentative chapter titles here)
VII. Summary and Conclusions

Preliminary Working Bibliography

Include in proper bibliographic form the references you have already examined, including those listed in the "Related Literature and Research section." This list should be comprehensive and up-to-date enough to show your reader you have delved into the problem and are aware of the sources available to complete your research. Show that you are acquainted with what has been done in the specific area you are investigating.

The following pages contain a sample proposal for a research project, Figure 3.1. A proposal for a thesis or dissertation could follow the same general format and include a review of related research. The main difference would likely be the depth and complexity of the elements included. Too, some supervising chairmen or committees may desire that the review of related literature and research be extensive and in nearly final form for a dissertation proposal. The student should determine committee preference before proceeding.

Evaluating the Research Proposal

The Problem and Its Development

The problem background information is pertinent and adequate to establish that a problem exists; there is a good transition to the problem statement; the problem statement is in question form and does not require a *yes* or *no* answer; the answer does not depend upon value judgments; the problem is factored into subproblems; and the subproblems are consistent and add to the overall problem. Hypotheses, if any, stem from the problem, and subproblems and are stated correctly, clearly, and simply. A need or purpose is established, not a mere repetition of the problem.

The Problem Amenities

Scope and limitations are differentiated: *scope* establishes problem boundaries and identifies exclusions as well as inclusions; *limitations* establish external handicaps imposed on the researcher. Review of related literature shows scope and depth in perspective and diligence in search, summarizes contributions, and has adequate documentation. Research methods and data sources are stated explicitly.

Proposal Support Material

The title is appropriate, clear, and concise. The working outline reflects depth in development, proper organization, and coordination of material; entries are clear and consistent with the research problem factoring. The working bibliography is current, comprehensive, and in proper format; it has reasonable balance of periodicals and books for the type of research.

The Written Presentation

Care and neatness are reflected in the overall presentation; the mechanics are consistent with the adopted style manual; writing style is smooth, interesting, and lucid; it has good diction, proper tense and person, and freedom from mechanical errors; it appears to be an in-depth treatment with an effort to perceive and answer reader questions or objections; explanations are full.

With the research design established and the proposal evaluated, your next step is the documentary sources search as described in Chapter 4.

FIGURE 3.1

Sample Research Proposal

AN EVALUATION OF PLANT LOCATION
CONSIDERATIONS FOR SELECTED
PHOENIX–AREA MANUFACTURERS

A Proposal
for a Research Project
in Partial Fulfillment
of the Requirements for the Course
Business Research Methods

Presented to
Dr. Charles B. Smith

by
Kenneth Megel

January 1986

FIGURE 3.1 (Continued)

Introduction

Phoenix and the Phoenix metropolitan area (Maricopa County) distinguished itself in the post-World War II period as one of the most rapidly expanding manufacturing centers of the Untied States. During 1940, a mere 322 manufacturing firms had operational facilities in all of Arizona.[1] These 332 firms comprised only two-tenths of one percent of the total 190,000 national manufacturing firms. By 1970, however, the number of manufacturers in the Phoenix metropolitan area alone had climbed to 1,097. A 220 percent growth rate had been established for Phoenix, while the national manufacturing total had grown only 64 percent to 311,000 firms within the same thirty-year period.[2]

The claim that manufacturing contributed significantly to Phoenix-area growth in the period 1945–71 is substantiated by data comparison. Between 1946 and 1970 the population of Arizona rose 188 percent, agricultural production rose 297 percent, mineral production rose 888 percent, and tourist expenditures rose 842 percent. Yet, during the same period, manufacturing output rose 2,456 percent. The 1970 dollar value of manufacturing output had been only 76 percent of mineral production.[3] While many areas of the Arizona economy were expanding with the postwar population boom, it was the inflow of new manufacturing facilities into Phoenix that established a base for the economic surge. If these trends continue, the economic growth of Phoenix in the 1980s will be integrally related to the ability of the Phoenix area to attract new industry. Before plans for the future can be formulated, however, a knowledge of the past must be gained.

FIGURE 3.1 (Continued)

Statement of the Problem

The problem confronting Phoenix economic planners and industrial developers that will be investigated in this research project is: Why did selected manufacturers choose to locate manufacturing facilities in the Phoenix area in 1984–85? This question generates two subquestions.

1. What factors did these manufacturers consider to be of major importance in their search for a plant location?
2. What did these manufacturers believe were the major advantages and disadvantages of locating in Phoenix?

A plant location decision differs in fundamental ways from other basic business functions because plant location projects are intermittent. Once under way, however, a location selection process overshadows all other decisions in its implications for the future. For this reason, a businessman is motivated to search for issues and to determine their future influence upon his proposed manufacturing facility. It is a businessman who has arrived at a location decision who is most qualified to analyze the relative strengths and weaknesses of the Phoenix area for manufacturing purposes.

Purpose of the Study

The primary purpose of this project will be to aid the business and economic community of Phoenix in its continuing attempt to attract new manufacturing firms to Phoenix. The economic and social appeal of Phoenix must be analyzed from a manufacturing point of view. The favorable qualities

FIGURE 3.1 (Continued)

may then be accentuated and remedial action applied to less favorable characteristics.

A secondary purpose of the study will be to assist executives of manufacturing firms that are considering locating a facility in the Phoenix area. Decision makers have faced comparable situations in the past. If a synthesis of their findings concerning Phoenix is available, the task facing the current analyst may become somewhat less formidable, and his reaction toward Phoenix may be favorably altered.

Scope of the Problem

This research project will be confined to the Phoenix, Arizona, metropolitan area. For the purpose of this project, the term "Phoenix metropolitan area" will be equated with the United States Department of Commerce term "Standard Metropolitan Statistical Area for Phoenix, Arizona" which is Maricopa County, Arizona.[4]

The study will be confined to manufacturing firms because the operational facilities and labor and tax considerations required by manufacturers differ in several ways from those of mining firms or service industries. The study will include only firms that have announced the location of and have completed the construction of their first manufacturing facility in the state of Arizona during 1984–85. This time span is chosen because of the rapidly changing nature of the manufacturing industry and the intensified growth of the Phoenix area since the early 1960s. An expansion of the time span involved could introduce factors that were important in the mid-1960s, but which had lost their major significance to manufacturers by 1983.

FIGURE 3.1 (Continued)

The study will be restricted to an analysis of factors leading toward the selection of one particular city (Phoenix) over another. No attempt will be made to determine the reasons for differentiation of one site within the city over another within Phoenix. Also, no attempt will be made to differentiate between purely economic considerations, which affect employee morale but not physical job conditions.

Limitations

The companies to be selected for participation will be chosen from the announcements of new manufacturing facilities in the Phoenix area in the 1984 and 1985 monthly issues of *Phoenix* magazine and *Arizona Modern Business and Industry*. These sources are dictated because a comprehensive listing of such new facilities is unavailable from either the Arizona Department of Economic Planning and Development or the Phoenix Chamber of Commerce. Project time constraints will prohibit a more intensive investigation through records of the Arizona Tax Commissioner. A preliminary survey shows that approximately thirty companies have announced as locating in Phoenix during the relevant time period.

No attempt will be made to speak to a specific person within each firm. The choice of the person to be interviewed will be left to the discretion of the receptionist after the nature of the research is explained.

Research Procedures

This research will differ mainly from past research in that this study will be conducted through personal interviews

FIGURE 3.1 (Continued)

and be restricted to newly located manufacturing firms in the Phoenix, Arizona, metropolitan area.

Secondary Source Data Collection

The research will be initiated by reviewing the available publications on manufacturing location. The following subject headings have been delineated for locating relevant articles:

Location of Industries	Location of Factories
Industrial Sites	Store Location
Business Removal	Location in Business
Industrial Management	Space in Economics
Labor Cost	Labor Turnover
Municipal Taxation	State Taxation
Transportation	Manufacturing

The data from business periodicals will be supplemented by a review of books available on manufacturing and economic location. The government documents section and the Arizona collection of the Hayden Library will provide the majority of statistical data about manufacturing in Phoenix. Phoenix promotional literature, Phoenix industrial site information, and Arizona tax data will be obtained through the Phoenix Chamber of Commerce and the Arizona Department of Economic Planning and Development. This secondary information will complement the primary data to be collected by interview. The collected data will be analyzed by factors that influenced manufacturers. No attempt will be made to differentiate between strictly economic factors involved and the more-difficult-to-evaluate psychological factors.

FIGURE 3.1 (Continued)

Primary Source Data Collection

The manufacturing firms will be contacted initially by telephone. The research will be explained to the telephone receptionist and an interview will be arranged with an executive of the firm at the discretion of the receptionist. At the time of the personal interview, the research project will be fully explained to the manufacturing executive. To ascertain the relevancy of the information presented in the interview, the first question to the interviewee will concern the extent of his actual involvement in the location selection procedure.

The actual interview guide has not been constructed at this point; it will include, however, these areas: (1) the factors that led the firm to select Phoenix as the site for the manufacturing facility; (2) the relative merits and shortcomings of the Phoenix area for each factor introduced; and (3) a ranking of a list of twenty factors that secondary literature has indicated were considered by manufacturers in a plant location analysis.

In addition to interviews with the manufacturing executives, interviews with officials for the Arizona Economic Planning and Development Department will be conducted in the same manner as mentioned for the manufacturers.

Tentative General Outline

I. Introduction
   A. Statement of the Problem
   B. Purpose of the Study
   C. Scope of the Problem

FIGURE 3.1 (Continued)

    D. Limitations
    E. Plan of Presentation
  II. Review of Related Literature and Research
    A. Selecting a General Type of Area
    B. Selecting a Particular City
 III. Research Procedures
    A. Secondary Source Data Collection
    B. Primary Source Data Collection
 IV. Determining the Major Location Factors
    A. Examining the Labor Supply
    B. Evaluating the Tax Structure
    C. Investigating the Market Accessibility
    D. Accessing Preproduction Factors
    E. Identifying Secondary Factors
  V. Evaluation the Attractiveness of Phoenix
    A. Labor Supply
    B. Tax Structure
    C. Market Accessibility
    D. Land and Construction Costs
    E. Climate and Water Availability
 VI. Conclusions and Recommendations
    A. Conclusions for Selected Manufacturers
    B. Recommendations for Further Research
    Appendices
    Bibliography

Preliminary Working Bibliography

(As mentioned, the actual bibliography as well as the footnotes are excluded from this example.)
    —Ken Megel, Arizona State University

4
Searching Documentary Sources

"**B**ut you, Daniel, shut up the words, and seal the book, even to the time of the end. Many shall run to and fro, and knowledge shall increase." This quotation from Daniel 12:4 characterizes some people's frantic search for material in the library—much running to and fro and much time wasted. No doubt a great many persons' library orientation has been weak or haphazard. So, your plan should be to become familiar with library reference sources, to develop a systematic plan for your documentary search, and to ask a librarian for help when you need it.

The purpose of this chapter is to introduce you to the various library sources of information and to show their relationships to the research project. Such documentary sources as books, periodicals, dissertations, theses, newspapers, letters, statistical abstracts, sound recordings, films, and the like are considered *secondary data sources.* Covered in this chapter are the following:

1. Noting documentary source terminology
2. Reviewing literature of the field
3. Developing a data collection plan
4. Collecting data from documentary sources
5. Evaluating the quality of secondary sources.

Noting Documentary Source Terminology

As it is in other aspects of the research process, precision in word choice and use is important in talking about and writing about library sources. A person who does not distinguish between *bibliography* and *index,* or between *index* and *table of contents,* or between *magazine* and *journal* lacks precision: and that person just may be careless in other aspects in treating secondary data.

An *index* is not a data source; it is an alphabetical *listing* of data sources and it tells only where the data can be found. A *bibliography,* though, is a specialized list of documentary sources giving author, title, and publication data, sometimes with an abstract of the source content; so, you compile a *bibliography* by consulting *indexes.* An *index* is not interchangeable with *table of contents* or *contents* in the research report. In this use, an *index* is an alphabetized list of subject matter in the report which includes the page numbers where it may be found. *Contents,* though, is an outline of the report presentation, with page numbers; it is a road map of the publication.

Although the terms *serial, journal, periodical,* and *magazine* are often used interchangeably, the careful writer would likely be more discriminating. A *journal* is a scholarly publication of a learned society or profession. *Serials* are publications that are issued at regular intervals, as are *periodicals* and *magazines.* But the term *magazine* now connotes the popular, newsstand type of publication. Thus, you would likely go to a *public serials list* in the library to obtain a listing and call numbers of journals, periodicals, magazines, and newspapers.

Microform is the label given to all photographically reduced reproductions of printed material, such as newspapers, journals, reports, and other such publications. *Microfilm* is strip film in 35mm and 16mm sizes. A *microcard* is an opaque reproduction of printed material and contains up to eighty pages of print on each card. *Microfiche* is similar to microcard except that it is a transparency. All microform material must be read on a reading machine, from which, on some machines, photographic prints can be made.

The search of documentary sources may sometimes require a twofold approach. For some research projects, the secondary data sources may provide all the data needed as specified by the research design. If your data source is thus confined to secondary data, you still have an obligation to review and report on the completed research related to the project you are undertaking. Therefore, the literature review, as described in the next section, applies to research using either primary data or secondary data.

Reviewing Literature of the Field

To review or search the literature means to examine the various indexes and card catalogs in libraries for information sources related to the problem selected. Seldom is one the first person to seek an answer to a particular problem. Very likely someone else has worked in the same area as you, and perhaps what they have done is so close to what you plan to undertake that you must take it into account to avoid duplication of effort. Thus, a literature search:

1. Helps to prevent a duplication of effort
2. Serves to orient readers on the status of the problem
3. Delinates major books and articles related to the problem
4. Relates significant opinions or perspectives about the problem area

5. Develops a rationale and the significance of the research; it indicates:
   a. the need for additional research
   b. the areas of conflict or areas of agreement or both
   c. the bases for challenging accepted ideas or views
6. Contributes to the research design
7. Furnishes evaluative techniques or criteria
8. Points out findings that will support or contrast with the findings of your study as will be described in your content chapters

The literature of the field, frequently called *related literature and research:* (1) should not merely repeat what those who are competent in the area already are likely to know; (2) should not be a string of quotations tied together with transitions; and (3) should not be a history of the field unless such a history can be justified by your problem statement. Even if a history is justified, it should appear elsewhere in the research report. The degree of relationship of the research reviewed should be discriminant and pertinent to your research as justified by one or more of the eight categories just listed. And, a reader should clearly understand the relationship between your study and the literature of the field. Further, one should see how your research will contribute to knowledge in your research area.

Although the difference between *related literature* and *related research* is clearly established, the two frequently are treated erroneously as one in theses and dissertations. Precision in description would require you to distinguish between the two. *Related literature* consists of writings from periodicals, journals, monographs, bulletins, and the like. This literature is made up of the authors' *ideas, beliefs,* and *descriptions* on a subject. *Related research,* however, is just what it says; it consists of completed *research* in the forms of theses, dissertations, and other formal research projects. This review of research may be synthesized from the research report itself or from articles reporting on the research as described in journal articles. Even so, of course, these articles may be only leads. You have an obligation to review the original source; you should not quote from the secondary source unless the original is unobtainable for review. Thus, both related literature and research may come from periodical articles, but only related research may come from research reports such as theses, dissertations, and independent research project reports.

The literature review is one of the steps in the orderly research process; so all research—even that stemming entirely from secondary sources—is expected to contain a treatment of related research. A research project that is based entirely on secondary data sources (the literature of the field), however, would not have a review of *related literature*; instead, a review of *related research* would be appropriate. You simply say what you mean and deliver what you promise.

What you have to say about the literature review depends, of course, upon the amount of such data available. For some projects, perhaps a diligent search will reveal very little or no related research. When this happens, you can do no more than describe that status. Your study then takes on added importance when little related research can be found. You would be on dangerous ground, however, to say, "No related material exists," because you certainly have not had the opportunity to examine *all* sources. Instead, report that "A diligent search has uncovered no related research."

Your review of related literature and research needs to reflect care in classification and organization of the data collected. Several bases are available for you to organize these data. Typical are:

1. A dichotomous basis of related literature and related research
2. An order of importance—from most important to least important in relationship to your study
3. An historical or time sequence
4. Important characteristics or criteria bases
5. A basis of major contribution to your research
6. Combinations of the foregoing bases

Whichever method you choose, just be sure the classification and relationships will be apparent to your reader and provide for his ease in reading and understanding. Remember, a person's judgment is no better than that person's information. Examples of related literature and research are shown in Chapter 7.

The foregoing review of related literature and research is essential in determining the research approach as was discussed in Chapter 3. The purpose of the next section is to provide some guides to help you in your review of literature and in your search for secondary data.

Developing a Data Collection Plan

Rather than to run frantically to and fro, you would do well to use a systematic approach in your documentary data search. Following are some guides.

1. See what is listed in the card catalog under your subject area. Note the subject headings listed at the bottom of each card. These headings will give you subdivisions and related headings for further searching.
2. Examine your subject area listing in the most recent *Business Periodicals Index* and *Public Affairs Information Service.* Also note the subdivisions. Work back through the earlier issues of the indexes.
3. Review guides to reference materials to note their suggestions for your subject area. For example, see the *Encyclopedia of Business Information Sources* or *How to Use the Business Library* by Johnson.
4. Look up your subject area in the *Subject Headings Used in the Dictionary Catalog of the Library of Congress.* This book gives subject headings and cross-references from possible related headings, as is described in a later sub-division of this chapter.
5. Examine bibliographies for possible source lists. Aside from asking the librarian for help, note especially *Bibliographic Index: A Cumulative Bibliography of Bibliographies. 1937—.*
6. As you examine books and periodicals, be alert for leads to additional sources as noted in their bibiliographies and references cited.

7. Look for research and research-related articles about your subject in such as *Dissertation Abstracts,* and the yearly bibliography published by the Associated University Bureaus of Business and Economic Research. Review also the research issues of the various journals.

8. Use the library call number of your subject area to browse in the stacks. Review contents pages and bibliographies in potentially useful books.

9. As you review, read, and browse, carry a supply of uniform-size bibliographic note cards with you. You may prepare your own note cards using Figure 4.1 as an example. The important thing is to be sure to obtain all the publication data of your source *right now.*

10. Ask someone who knows—a specialist—for suggestions. Do not place *complete* reliance on the specialist, however, because that person just *may* have gaps in knowledge.

Collecting Data from Documentary Sources

The serious student will find the card catalog is the most important resource in the library. The card catalog, a systematic listing of books and materials in the library, provides an index to most of the library holdings. The materials not listed here may be found through use of separate indexes, such as government documents, pamphlets, and articles in periodicals. Thus, the card catalog is suggested as a first checkpoint in the data search, followed by a review of reference guides. A comprehensive listing of documentary sources is provided in Appendix A.

Evaluating the Quality of Secondary Sources

Collecting data from secondary sources requires careful selection of what you will record. Indiscriminate, voluminous note taking from all sources likely means you will have to discard much of it for actual use because it would not be of acceptable quality for a research project. Collect data with the premise that all data you use in testing an hypothesis will

FIGURE 4.1

Student-Prepared Note Card

Library call number _____

Author _____

Book or article title _____ Pages _____

Name of Periodical _____ Month, day, year _____

Book Publisher _____ City _____ Year _____

Edition, editor, etc. _____

have to be defended. You may be asked some very penetrating questions about your data and analysis.

Depending upon the nature of the research, the criteria for evaluating secondary data will vary. Mainly, you will be concerned with the following factors: reliability, accuracy, coverage, author qualification, and the nature of the publication.

Reliability

Secondary data reliability is dependent upon such factors as impartiality and timeliness. You should evaluate data in terms of its recency. What is the book copyright date? How much time has elapsed between the author's data collection and the publication date?

How free from bias are the data? Is the author likely to have a special reason to make a case for a biased point of view to the exclusion of all negative data? What is the relevancy of the data to that which you are seeking?

Reliability may be partly determined by the author-publisher combination. How authoritative the data are can be indicated for textbooks by the number of editions, which is related to acceptance in the field.

Accuracy

An evaluation of accuracy sometimes requires cross-checks with other sources. You should be concerned with such factors as whether the author distinguishes between fact and opinion and whether the sources are documented. Did the data come from other documents, surveys, and experiments, or from the author's experience? How ready would you be to accept the following statements without documentation or evidence for their derivation?

> Eighty percent of the scientists who have ever lived are alive today.

> Each year, Washington generates more than two billion pieces of paper—ten different forms for every man, woman, and child in the country and enough to fill Yankee Stadium from the playing field to the top of the stand fifty-one times.

Also, is the document an original or has it been edited? Has it been condensed? Was it ghostwritten?

Coverage

Review the table of contents of books you select in your search to determine the scope of the material and the amount of detail. Skim an article or book for perspective. Is it superficial with only broad generalizations? Is it lean, with a handbook or guidance approach? Is it a philosophical approach with great detail?

Author Qualification

The title page usually relates the author's profession or business and standing, and the preface of a book often gives the author's reason for writing. These factors, along with the quality of writing evident to you, give you a basis for appraising the author.

Nature of the Publication

What is the reputation of the publisher? Is the publisher noted for quality manuscript selection? If it is a periodical, is it an academic or professional journal, a trade magazine, or a popular magazine? If it is an academic or professional journal, how are manuscripts reviewed? Who is on the editorial board?

Overall, if you have any special comment about the data you select, you should so state during your data analysis in the content chapters. Some of the criteria discussed in this section also will apply to primary data collection, as is described next in Chapter 5.

5

Collecting Survey Data

At this stage of the investigation, you now have established the research problem, built a research design, and reviewed the literature; so the emphasis now shifts to data collection through survey techniques.

Discussed in this chapter are:

1. Noting data qualities
2. Developing and using the questionnaire
3. Structuring and conducting the interview
4. Making observations
5. Noting sampling considerations

Noting Data Qualities

Survey (primary) data are those data that do not yet exist; they come into being as the researcher collects them. As was mentioned in Chapter 1, primary data are collected (1) by survey through a questionnaire, an interview, or observation, or (2) by an experiment.

Data may be classified by qualities as *subjective* or *objective*. Subjective data are affected by a person's perceptions, beliefs, or whims. Data collected through observation is subjective; we do not see or perceive events in the same manner. Objective data come from those agreed-upon measuring devices that permit people to arrive at the same answer. A meter scale, a thermometer, a cash register, and some tests provide objective data. Measuring a person's height with a meter scale will provide objective data. Measuring that person's moral growth will provide subjective data.

Also, the qualities of *reliability* and *validity* are important in data collection. Simply, *reliability* is the degree of stability attributed to a measure derived from a sample of a population about which we wish to generalize. Significance or significance of a difference may be a more appropriate term in some situations, such as for value judgments about the measures and reliability for statistical probabilities of obtaining similar results in further testing. The desired quality, then, is that measuring instruments measure with reasonable uniformity; they should be as reliable as possible. If you were to measure your desk with a meter scale today, you would expect to obtain the same measurements of the desk tomorrow (negating persistent, sampling, or human error). Suppose you administered a vocational aptitude test to a person and the results showed a high aptitude for clerical-type work. If this same test were administered to the same person a few weeks later, and the new results showed a high aptitude for manual skills work, we would say the test was not very reliable.

Validity is the degree to which an instrument measures what it purports to measure. We accept the meter scale as a valid measure of distance or the clock as a valid measure of time. But if we devise a test to measure a person's self-concept of his ability in mathematics, how do we know whether the test actually measures that ability? An instrument may measure some *thing* reliably (with stability) but we may not be sure *what* thing. Obviously, then, we have to compare the measurements from an instrument to accepted

criteria for the thing being measured. When we move to measure human traits or qualities, such as honesty, patriotism,
loyalty, or aggression, comparison criteria are difficult to obtain.

As mentioned, primary data come from surveys and experiments. Experiments, however, are mainly a concern of research design and method: thus, the emphasis here is on collecting data through the use of questionnaires, interviews,
and observations.

Developing and Using the Questionnaire

Perhaps one of the most used and abused methods of data collection is the questionnaire. Carelessness in questionnaire
construction and not fulfilling promises made to respondents
have contributed to the questionnaire's poor reputation. Such
carelessness—and ignorance—in questionnaire construction
is evidenced by a person's developing a questionnaire before
the problem statement has been set out. When you consider
the function of a questionnaire, how can you logically construct a questionnaire before you have identified and stated
the research problem? Survey questionnaires are often observed to contain questions whose answers make no contribution toward answering the apparent research problem and
whose answers do not appear in the data presentation and analysis sections of the final report. Inclusion of such questions
suggests fuzzy thinking in questionnaire construction.

Thus, to collect data through the use of a questionnaire,
you should:

1. State the problem and subproblems (or factors). A helpful practice is to write each subproblem on a three-by-
   five-inch card. These statements can become the major
   headings or divisions of the questionnaire.
2. Develop questions whose answers will contribute to
   the answers of each subproblem listed on the foregoing
   heading cards.
3. Consider questions that will furnish bases for noting
   trends and relationships; determining economic, social,

or political values; noting causes and effects; meeting established standards; and determining relationships with current opinion or belief.

4. Sort these individual cards into groups headed by the cards named in step 1. Thus, each of these discussion areas should yield its subordinate questions to permit answering the overall research question and provide a basis for analysis for meaning.

Such preliminary work in developing a questionnaire pays off for you by providing for organization of questions before the rough-draft stage; easy revision of questions; help in layout or format; and assurance that all questions contribute to the problem answer—that a question has not been asked merely because it would be nice to know. The foregoing discussion of questionnaire construction is shown graphically in Figure 5.1.

Following are some helpful hints and guides for constructing the questionnaire.

General

1. Do you have your research problem well formulated and factored?
2. Is the questionnaire method the best possible way of getting the desired information?
3. Are you asking for information that you could obtain from available records?
4. Is the subject worth investigation, and will the respondents consider it worth their time to answer the questionnaire?
5. Is the questionnaire of such a length that the recipients may be reasonably expected to give the amount of time necessary for accurate answers?
6. Are the respondents likely to be willing or be authorized to supply the answers to your questions?
7. Do the questions stimulate supplementary comments and provide a basis for analysis rather than mere fact grubbing?

8. Is the purpose clear and with definite limits? Does each item of information fit into a pattern of essential knowledge about the problem?
9. Have you obtained the critical reactions of others who are familiar with questionnaire methods? Have you reviewed textbooks on research techniques for additional help?

FIGURE 5.1

Questionnaire Development

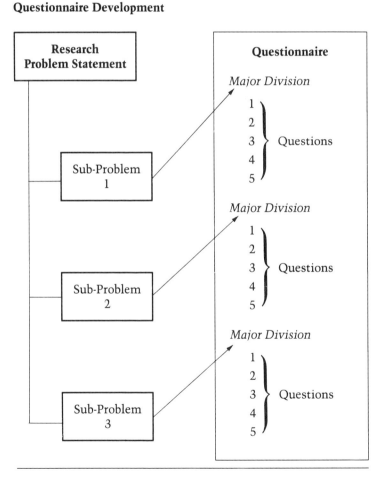

Form

1. Is the size proper for handling and filing?
2. Do you have enough identifying material in a conspicuous position at the top of the questionnaire?
3. Are the spacing and type conducive to ease in filling out the questionnaire and in such position that none will be omitted?
4. Are the spaces for answers near the right-hand or left-hand margin or in some other place where they will be easy to tabulate?
5. Is the general appearance, neatness, and character of the questionnaire designed to encourage complete and accurate answers? Carelessly prepared questionnaires are likely to elicit careless answers.
6. If the questionnaire is set up for coding, is ample room left so that the respondent will not feel cramped? Consider these aids: checklist, rating system, control codes for classifying questions and responses.
7. Have you guaranteed the anonymity of respondents or confidentiality of responses?
8. Have you constructed questions so that the answers will lend themselves to tabulation and statistical treatment?
9. Do the questions have parallel grammatical construction?
10. Is your address on the questionnaire so that you may get it back if the return envelope is lost?
11. Have you used headings to identify major divisions of the questionnaire?
12. Will the paper take ink?
13. Have you left enough blank space to permit binding of pages in the completed research report?
14. Will the questionnaire, when folded conventionally, fit the enclosed return envelope?

Selection and Arrangement of Items

1. Are all unusual or technical terms so defined that uniform interpretations will be received? Define with the question.
2. Are the questions so framed that they can be answered with a minimum amount of writing?

3. Are the questions so clear that only one interpretation is possible?
4. If facts are requested, is it clear whether exact or estimated answers are wanted? If opinions are requested, is their probable value assured?
5. Do questions appear in logical order so as to stimulate interest and facility in answering?
6. Have the questions been tried out on a sampling of the group to whom they will be sent?
7. Are the questions easy to answer, but still designed to get the required information?
8. Have all trivial questions and those which are not absolutely essential been weeded out?
9. Have you checked for biased or loaded questions? Are you forcing a particular answer?
10. Do fixed alternative (multiple choice) answers provide for the full range of possible replies?
11. Is any question's answer likely to be influenced by the content of a preceding question?
12. Can diagrams, charts, etc. be included to facilitate or clarify response?
13. Have questions been worded in such a way that they can be answered simply by a checkmark?
14. Have you avoided the use of words that are susceptible to different interpretations: e.g., moral or immoral, good or bad, rich or poor, intelligent or ignorant, laborer or capitalist?
15. Have you placed detailed questions toward the end of the questionnaire?
16. Have you inserted questions to serve as a check on other questions? For example, "age" may be checked by "date of birth."
17. Does any question require unnecessary mathematical calculations?

Mailing and Follow-up

1. Are the questionnaires mailed so that they are likely to reach the respondents at a time convenient for them to answer?

2. Does a clear, honest, neat covering letter make a courteous appeal to the interest of the addressee? Does it have a professional appearance? (A checklist follows this section.)
3. Is a stamped, addressed return envelope enclosed?
4. Have follow-up letters or phone calls been used?
5. What percentage of the returns were received? What effect would those that were not returned have upon the total picture?
6. Have you fulfilled promises and commitments made to the respondents?

Cover or Transmittal Letter

1. Use an inductive-type opening paragraph. A challenging question that cannot be answered yes or no is a good choice. Whet the reader's interest from the start. Avoid the bland, stereotyped opening, such as, "I am a graduate student at Blank University and I have selected as my research topic. . . ."
2. Encourage response by your choice of words. Make completion of the questionnaire sound easy and of benefit to the respondent.
3. Promise confidentiality if that truly is what you will do. Do not try subterfuge devices such as pin pricks, pencil dots, invisible ink, and other such coding devices. Aside from the ethical considerations, these devices sometimes backfire on the researcher.
4. Ask confidently for the questionnaire completion and return by a certain date so you can meet your deadline. Then close with a first person, future tense expression of appreciation.

See, for example, how the foregoing principles are applied in the sample cover letter, Figure 5.2.

Structuring and Conducting the Interview

The flexibility of the structured interview can yield better information than that from the questionnaire. Interviewing

FIGURE 5.2

Sample Cover Letter

March 23, 1989

Mr. William J. Gray
Director of Personnel
American Fidelity Company
Baltimore, Maryland 21233

Dear Mr. Gray:

To what extent is Job Enrichment currently being used in the insurance industry? To answer this question, I am currently engaged in research to update the 1975 study in which your company participated.

The 1975 study was reported in the article "Job Enlargement in Insurance Companies," *Best Insurance News*, Life Edition, June 1976. And, as before, the information provided by your company will be held in strict confidence; returned questionnaires will be used for statistical summaries only. A copy of the findings and conclusions will be mailed to you upon completion of the study.

Preliminary research has shown that the Personnel Department is typically the best qualified to complete the enclosed questionnaire. If you do not have the necessary information, please pass it along to the proper person.

To insure correct analysis of the data, completed questionnaires are needed from all the companies in the sample. Even though your company currently may not be using Job Enrichment, please answser the appropriate questions and return the questionnaire in the postage-paid envelope.

I shall appreciate your cooperation in the conduct of this research by your returning the completed questionnaire before April 10.

Cordially,

A. Researcher
Project Director

permits rephrasing of questions to assure understanding and permits requesting clarification of answers, neither of which is possible with the questionnaire. And, from this standpoint, the interview is similar to the observation method of data collection. Thus, without geographical or monetary constraints, the interview would be the best choice for collecting primary data as compared with the questionnaire. Of course, aside from the two constraints mentioned, the questionnaire can sometimes gain access to a person or an office where an interviewer could not.

Potential interviewer errors come mainly from the following three sources:

1. Errors in stimulating responses. Sometimes the interviewer's manner, facial expression, or explanations will bias the interviewee's answer.
2. Errors in handling nonresponse. The nonresponse group cannot be considered representative of the responding group. Failure to include those who refuse to answer certain questions or are not at home (working vs unemployed) may bias the sample.
3. Errors in recording and interpreting responses. The cultural background of the interviewer may affect how a response is recorded (what he expected or hoped to hear) and how it is interpreted. And, the interviewer's experience and attitude such as that stemming from inadequate training or wages may affect recording and interpretation.

The following checklist contains suggestions for planning and conducting the interview.

General

1. Do you have your research problem well formulated and factored?
2. Have you selected the right person to interview? Will that person have the information? Will he or she have the authority to divulge it, and be willing to do so?
3. Have you determined how many people you need to interview to serve as a basis for valid generalizations?

4. Have you informed the respondent about the nature of the project, told why cooperation is needed, and motivated the person to cooperate?
5. Should you give the interviewee a copy of your interview guide to facilitate answering?

Interview Plan and Questions

1. Will you be prepared to record unexpected data?
2. Have you conducted pilot interviews outside the interview sample, but with people similar to the sample respondents?
3. Do you know how much time the interview is likely to take?
4. Have you listed the questions you will ask? Have you considered using a check-list of possible answers to facilitate your recording answers?

Arranging the Interview

1. Have you arranged for the interview through a letter, telephone call, mutual friend, or a letter of introduction?
2. Have you set a definite time and place for the interview satisfactory to the respondent—one that will avoid rush periods in the day, week, or month?
3. Will you be likely to have privacy to encourage confidential answers?

Conducting the Interview

1. Develop a cordial atmosphere through conversation; perhaps talk about the respondent. Help the interviewee feel at ease. Do not lead off with unpleasant or emotion-loaded topics.
2. Avoid the "investigation" or "third-degree" approach.
3. Ask one question at a time; let the person answer fully. Give an opportunity to qualify an answer. Be alert for the need to repeat the answer to see whether it was the answer intended. Be alert for inaccuracies. Listen for casual remarks; watch facial expressions.

4. Avoid displaying surprise, shock, or disinterest at an answer.
5. Do not embarrass the respondent or reflect a superior, know-it-all attitude.
6. Dress appropriately for the situation.
7. Do not let your note taking interrupt the person's answers.
8. Stay within the alloted time period for your interview unless you are invited to stay longer.
9. Promise anonymity or privileged treatment of data when necessary.

After the Interview

1. Send the respondent a letter of thanks for cooperating and contributing to your study—if this is reasonable considering the number of interviews conducted.
2. Maintain a list of interviews, places, and dates. Use these items for thank-you letters and for your footnotes and bibliography.
3. Complete and consolidate your information immediately after the interview.

Making Observations

The observation method is useful: (1) when you must classify or determine people's characteristics, their actions, or frequency and effects of their actions; and (2) when you must count incidents, people, vehicles, and the like. Observation is a very useful method in social research, such as determining the effectiveness of a sales training program or in determining how salespeople treat customers.

The observation method leads to description—and every word in the description means *something*. Therefore, precision in word choice and careful use of definitions are important in recording the description. In general, observations are recorded in the following ways: (1) check-lists; (2) rating scales; (3) periodic summaries, such as the "critical incident" technique; and (4) photographic record. An observer should:

1. Know and be able to identify the specific elements that are to be observed. This ability implies adequate training and instruction.
2. Record the observations immediately.
3. Observe an established number of incidents or cases.
4. Check the recorded observations for accuracy and completeness.

Further, the observer should be aware of the following limitations in the observation method:

1. If people know they are being observed, they may alter their behavior.
2. Some events may be spontaneous; so the observer may not be there to observe. Or, the interval between events may be so long that the observer cannot always be available.
3. Some extraneous factors that may hinder observations cannot be controlled: e.g., weather, presence of another person.
4. Repeat observations may be impractical or impossible.
5. Observations are subject to the observer's values and interpretations in recording observations. The situation may require using a jury system for making the observation and then using the jury consensus.

Noting Sampling Considerations

The use of sampling is a major tool in conducting effective research. Therefore, the knowledge and proper use of sampling is extremely important in developing a research design. Samples are used widely in research because of certain general advantages of the techniques: (1) Savings are made possible. Interviewing or testing costs are substantially the same per person interviewed or tested. (2) A sample's small size makes it possible to collect sample data more quickly than census data (complete enumeration). (3) For several classes of problems, sampling is the only practicable method. Some testing procedures involve destroying the item being tested.

The tensile strength of rope is tested by stretching a piece of it until it breaks. A light bulb's life is determined by burning it until it fails. So, when testing consists of ultimate destruction, one must sample to find the properties of the *universe* or have no universe left after testing.

Sampling is used, for example, in consumer surveys, surveys of attitudes and opinions, statistical problems in accounting and auditing, and appraising property. The government is actively involved in sampling. Every month the government gives figures on the cost of living, employment, retail sales, and prices. Important economic decisions then are made by government and industry based on statistics derived from using sampling techniques.

Sampling Terminology

One cannot talk about sampling without having an understanding of the following terms. A *population* or *universe* is the total of all things being studied at one time; it is the complete set of possible measurements. For example, a population may be all students currently enrolled in accredited four-year colleges and universities in Arizona.

A *sample* is a part of the population or universe selected for examination. A sample is *representative* if its characteristics approximate very closely the population characteristics. A sample is *random* when it is selected without bias. Thus, each item in the population has an equal or specified opportunity to be selected for the sample. Then, through this sample, we can generalize about the population. Synonomous with random sample is a *probability* sample. Technically, we could say we have a probability sample because it was selected through random choices.

The probability that other similarly selected samples would yield similar values is called *level of confidence.* Usually it is given in terms of the number of standard deviations away from a percentage or mean. The *standard deviation* is a measure of the variation within a set of data. Other measures of variation are available, but the standard deviation is the one used most frequently.

The standard deviation is derived by: (1) obtaining the

mean of the set of data, (2) noting the deviation of *each* observation in the set of data from the mean of the set, (3) adding the squares of the deviations, (4) dividing by the number of observations, and (5) taking the square root of the mean of the squared deviations.

When the standard deviation for a sample is known, we can make a rigorous statistical statement about the extent to which a mean derived from the sample is representative of the true mean. We can say, in effect, that a difference exists between the obtained mean and the true mean. We can further say that we are 68 percent confident that our sample mean is within one standard deviation of the true mean. If we wish to be 95 percent confident, we can use two standard deviations, and if we want to be 99 percent sure, we can use three standard deviations.

By establishing confidence intervals, we can make judgments about the mean based on a percentage of confidence.

Considering Sampling Techniques and Sample Size

The first step in selecting a sample is to delineate carefully the population to be studied and the characteristics to be analyzed. The sample selected must be of adequate size and must be representative to prevent distortion. The particular sampling technique you choose will depend upon the characteristics of the population being surveyed. Each sampling technique has its advantages in certain situations and its limitations in others. Your main task in designing a sample is to select the technique best suited for your problem and to adapt this technique to any special conditions of your research design. The intent for this presentation is to furnish only a general understanding of sampling. You are encouraged to consult a specialized text or texts and articles on sampling and statistics. Suggested sources are provided in Appendix A.

Sampling Techniques

Samples are generally classified on the basis of how the items are chosen from the population to be part of the sample. On this basis, samples are classified into three broad types: (1) convenience samples, (2) judgment samples, and (3) probability samples.

Convenience samples. Convenience samples are the simplest of all sample types. These are identified by the fact that the universe items making up the sample are selected by taking those items most readily available. Sometimes this sampling method is labeled an *accidental sample;* yet, the design may be intentional as dictated by time or convenience of access to the universe items.

Judgment samples. In a judgment-type sample, sometimes called a *purposive* or *quota sample,* the basis for selecting items rests upon the experience and judgment of the selector. Usually this selector is an expert in the subject field involved in the study. Thus, the sample items are deliberately chosen from the universe. Although samples of this type may be subject to relatively small errors if the expert's judgment is good, the errors still cannot be measured or predicted.

Probability samples. A *probability sample* is one that has been so selected that quantitatively measurable statistical inferences can be made about the degree of representativeness of the sample data. The selection process implies lack of direction—selection is independent of the person making the study and selecting the sample. Randomness can be achieved in a number of ways. For example, tables are available that have lists of random numbers, a computer may generate random numbers, or you may select every nth item in a list and thereby achieve a random sample. The key to random sampling is the realization that in using this method all the individuals in the universe have a known chance of being selected for the sample; so the results of one sample can be tested by the laws of probability. Only then can we draw really rigorous inferences about the population from the data of the sample.

Among the probability-sample-types are *stratified, systematic, area, cluster,* and *sequential analysis.*

A *stratified* sample is derived by dividing the population into homogenous sub-groups and then selecting a sample from each sub-group. For example, a university student body could be divided into sub-groups based on the characteristics of class standing—freshman, sophomore, junior, senior, masters, and doctorate. This stratified sample is *proportionate* when the sample number selected from each sub-group is proportionate to the total number in the population.

Systematic sampling is a process choosing the items for a sample by using a predetermined numerical plan, such as selecting every first, third, fifth, or tenth item. This method eliminates human bias and can be used in conjunction with other sampling techniques.

An *area* sample results when geographic location determines the population to be sampled. The factors of representativeness, probability, and human bias must be considered as in other sampling techniques.

Cluster sampling results when sample targets are selected in groups rather than singly. This method reduces cost but increases the margin for error.

Sequential analysis sampling is a data collection technique that has built-in mechanisms to determine when adequate results have been achieved and the survey can be discontinued.

Sample size. In general, the sample size needed is dependent upon the purpose of the study and the characteristics (variability) of the population studied. A sample considered adequate for one purpose may be inadequate for other purposes. This is true because, statistically, the adequacy of a sample depends upon:

1. The characteristics of the population
2. The precision required or desired
3. The cost of gathering the data
4. The cost of risk associated with a wrong conclusion or wrong decision.

Statistical theory and principles are practically the same in all types of applications, but the population and the stated use of the data are different. The merits of a sample, then, must be evaluated in view of these differences. What is considered an adequate sample in one instance may be inadequate in another instance. Before passing judgment on the merits of a sample, the user of the sampled data should consider the purpose for which the data will be used and the nature of the population studied in addition to statistical theory, principles, and formulas.

In view of the foregoing, an adequate sample is defined as:

1. A small-scale replica of the population studied,
2. sufficiently precise for the stated uses,
3. with the sampling error reduced to an acceptable margin to avoid leading someone to a wrong conclusion or wrong decision, and
4. with the cost of the sample, plus the cost or risk associated with a wrong conclusion or wrong decision, minimized.

An abundance of techniques for determing sample size may be found in the literature, and the researcher should examine these sources to select an appropriate method.

Being Aware of Ethics in Research

Following are some considerations or issues involving ethics in research. Some of the statements are based upon items in professional codes of ethics from the American Marketing Association, the American Psychological Association, the American Sociological Association, and the Operations Research Society. The treatment in this section is intended only to show the breadth of concern among professional organizations for the conduct of researchers. The frequently mentioned concerns are:

- Using pretense of research as a means of making contact for sales purposes.
- Violating promise of confidentiality or anonymity by use of hidden coding on survey instruments.

- Using one-way mirrors without respondent's knowledge or permission.
- Requiring involuntary participation; coercing the participants, such as implying a questionnaire survey needs to be completed to register a product guarantee.
- Using fake long-distance phone calls to make contact with a respondent.
- Asking questions that are too personal.
- Disguising the name of the research sponsor.
- Promising respondent a summary of the research results to get cooperation but with no intention to follow through.
- Using a role as a researcher to obtain information for other than professional purposes.
- Not protecting participants from physical or mental discomfort or harm.
- Using long, technical appendices or technical jargon or both in written or oral presentations to mislead the recipient on the thoroughness of the job or the researcher's competence.
- Not maintaining scientific objectivity.
- Publishing research conclusions that are inconsitent or not warranted by the data.
- Omitting data from a report that might significantly modify the interpretation of the findings.
- Not disclosing sources of financial support.
- Not acknowledging research assistance or collaboration.

In summary, effective research in many areas requires a knowledge of survey and sampling techniques and an awareness of the ethics involved. The proper use of these techniques is essential because the ramifications of conclusions reached through them may have far-reaching effects. With primary data collection methods established, Chapter 6, next, contains a discussion of data organization, classification, and outlining.

6
Developing the Outline

Roots, wood, bark, and leaves singly perfect may be;
But clapt hodge-podge together, they don't make a tree.
—James Russell Lowell, "A Fable for Critics"

And so it is with a research report. All the parts set out hodge-podge don't make a report. If you are to make a coherent presentation, you need to organize and outline your material. Just as you need a map to take a long trip, so do you need a plan to follow in presenting data. In this chapter are discussed:

1. Noting the nature of an outline
2. Organizing the data
3. Constructing the outline
4. Evaluating the outline
5. Using typographical gradations

The Nature of an Outline

The outline is the skeleton that holds your report together. It gives your presentation a sense of continuity, of unity or coherence; and it is the final step before writing. You may have done an exceptional job in developing and carrying out your research; but if your written presentation is such that your reader cannot get the information out, you can hide your efforts completely. Unfortunately, the converse is not true. An exceptional written presentation opens the window wide for your reader to see in; so if the research effort is poor, it becomes readily apparent. Remember, a major consideration is not how you can conveniently put all the information *in* your report, but how easy it will be for your reader to get the information *out*. Your reader expects to find the information in a logical order, such as 1-2-3-4-5, not 1-3-2-5-4.

An illogical presentation causes your reader to question, to back up and reread, and to be irritated. We are frustrated by disorder. When we encounter disorder, we are annoyed by it or we try to withdraw from it, or both. Outlining, properly done, is a method of obviating disorder. It is a method of dividing so that all the parts must add up to the whole.

Relationship of the Outline to the Report

To understand the nature of an outline, we need to see its relationship to the research report. This relationship becomes evident when the research report parts are delineated. These report parts fall into three major divisions: (1) prefatory material, (2) report body, and (3) appended material. These divisions may be further divided as:

Prefatory material	Report body	Appended material
title page	introduction	appendixes
acceptance page	review of literature	bibliography or references cited
abstract	methods	
acknowledgments	data and analysis (the content chapters)	
table of contents	conclusions and recommendations	
list of tables		
list of illustrations		

The final outline, with the addition of page numbers, becomes a part of the "Table of Contents." That is, the "Table of Contents" contains a listing of some prefatory material, the report body, and the appended material. But logically an outline is confined to the report body. You can classify, organize, and outline the data you have collected. Thus, the relationship becomes:

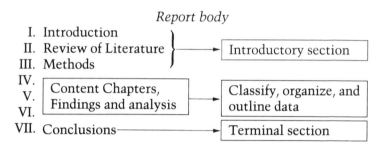

Therefore, in the foregoing example, I, II, III, and VII are not *logical* parts of an outline. Custom, however, has conferred coordinate status to those parts; so, we include introductory material and terminal material in the outline.

Types of Outlines

Two outline systems are in general use—*alpha numeric* and *numeric* (or *decimal*). The alpha-numeric system uses Roman and Arabic numerals combined with upper- and lower-case letters in a descending order of importance. In the numeric system, sometimes called the decimal system, Arabic numerals only are used. An example of the two systems is shown in Figure 6.1.

Usually the suggestions in style manuals are that the degree of subheadings be shown by typographical gradations rather than by number or alpha-numeric notation. Therefore, select the outline system with which you feel most comfortable because the outline number or alphabet notations are not carried over into the final report draft.

FIGURE 6.1

**An Example of Alpha-numeric and
Numeric Outlining Systems**

	Alpha-numeric	Numeric
First Major Division Heading	I.	1.
First-degree subheading	A.	1.11
First-degree subheading	B.	1.12
Second-degree subheading	1.	1.21
Second-degree subheading	2.	1.22
Third-degree subheading	a)	1.31
Third-degree subheading	b)	1.32
Fourth-degree subheading	(1)	1.41
Fourth-degree subheading	(2)	1.42
Fifth-degree subheading	(a)	1.51
Fifth-degree subheading	(b)	1.52
Second Major Division Heading	II.	2.
First-degree subheading	A.	2.11
First-degree subheading	B.	2.12
Second-degree subheading	1.	2.21
Second-degree subheading	2.	2.22
Third-degree subheading	a)	2.31
Third-degree subheading	b)	2.32
Fourth-degree subheading	(1)	2.41
Fourth-degree subheading	(2)	2.42
Fifth-degree subheading	(a)	2.51
Fifth-degree subheading	(b)	2.52

For either system of outlining, you may choose one of four styles—*word, phrase, sentence,* or *paragraph*—for building the outline. Of the four, the *phrase* style most readily lends itself to the construction techniques discussed in this chapter. The *word* style leads to vagueness and generality, and the *sentence* and *paragraph* styles become rather cumbersome to manipulate using techniques to be discussed later. For example, a section of an outline from a study on converting to a computerized inventory control system might look like this for word and phrase styles:

Word Style	*Phrase Style*
V. Operation	V. Operating the Computerized System
A. Reliability	A. Obtaining Reliability
1. Schedule	1. Planning a realistic schedule
2. Adjustment	2. Adjusting to perturbations
B. Accuracy	B. Considering Accuracy of Operation
C. Cost	C. Determining Cost of Operation
D. Personnel	D. Evaluating Personnel Problems

The Principle of Outline Division

The principle or logic of outlining is that of division. Therefore, like arithmetic, all outline parts must add to the whole. Logically, I + II + III + IV + V should add to the research problem.

I.	Introduction
II. ⎫	Content Chapters
+ III. ⎬	Data and Analysis
+ IV. ⎭	
V.	Conclusion

In the example shown here, however, I and V are the "Introduction" and "Conclusion"; therefore, they are not logical parts of the outline. They do not add to the research problem because they do not contain data and analysis that contribute to the answer, as was mentioned previously.

For a major division, such as III in the foregoing example, the A, B, C under III must equal what is promised in III. That is, III = A + B + C. Further, the divisions under A, B, and C must total what is promised for each, or A = 1 + 2 + 3. The same principle operates for all outline divisions.

Organizing the Data

To organize data means: (1) to divide the data on the basis of some relationship or common denominator and (2) to arrange the data in some logical or natural order.

You already have begun the division process by factoring your research problem. The sub-questions you derived by factoring will likely be the major content divisions in your outline. For example:

II. Sub-question 1
III. Sub-question 2 (recast the sub-questions
IV. Sub-question 3 into chapter titles)

All these major divisions in the data presentation should reflect a common denominator, such as characteristics, criteria, functions, conditions, uses, or forms. For example:

Characteristics	*Functions*
II. Labor Supply	II. Initiating the System Study
III. Market Accessibility	III. Designing the System
IV. Tax Structure	IV. Installing the Computerized System

The next step is to arrange the data in some logical or natural order. You derive a *logical order* on the basis of your reasoning, whereas *natural order* is intrinsic in the subject. Generally, these bases serve for arranging data:

place or space   simple to complex
time or sequence   general to specific
qualitative   specific to general
quantitative   increasing or decreasing
problem-solution   order of importance
pro-con   cause-effect or effect-cause
pleasant-unpleasant

Whatever basis you select for arranging the major divisions, you are likely to use a different basis for the subhead-

ings. Thus, an outline has at least two organization bases involved.

Constructing the Outline

At this point, a review of some of the principles and examples set out in earlier chapters is appropriate. This review
will show how those principles contribute to your outline
construction. Figure 3.1, the sample research proposal, involves plant location considerations. The researcher's
thought processes for this research probably went something like this:

1. "I wonder why those manufacturers who located in
   Phoenix chose Phoenix." Then, using the principles
   outlined in Figures 2.1 and 2.2, the researcher developed
   a conditional statement like this:
2. "I can determine why those manufacturers who located
   in Phoenix chose Phoenix:
   by 1. determining what factors those manufacturers
           considered important in their search for a plant
           location *and*
   by 2. determining what those manufacturers believed
           were the major advantages and disadvantages of
           locating in Phoenix."
3. Next, the researcher cast those statements into research-
   problem format. In doing so, he worked in the restrictive
   elements to confine the scope of his work, thus: "Why
   did selected manufacturers choose to locate their manufacturing facilities in the Phoenix area in 1984–85?" That
   is:

   1. What factors did these manufacturers consider to be
      of major importance in their search for a plant loca-
      tion?
   2. What did these manufacturers believe were the major
      advantages and disadvantages of locating in Phoenix?
4. Through his preliminary investigation and his reviewing the literature and research, he determined the ex-

pected location factors and factors pertinent to Phoenix. With this information he built a tentative outline:

I. Introduction
II. Review of Related Literature and Research
III. Research Procedures
IV. Major Location Factors
    A. Labor Supply
+ B. Market Availability
+ C. Tax Structure
+ D. Pre-Production Factors
+ E. Secondary Factors = Major Location Factors
V. Phoenix Factors
    A. Labor Supply
+ B. Market Availability
+ C. Tax Structure
+ D. Land and Construction Costs
+ E. Climate and Water Availability = Phoenix Factors
VI. Conclusions

5. The researcher then applied some tests to his outline such as have been discussed so far:

—IV and V (content chapters) are both *characteristics,* the common denominator.

—IV and V add to the answer to the research problem.

—A + B + C + D + E add to what is promised in the caption for IV.

—A + B + C + D + E add to what is promised in the caption for V.

6. After the researcher collected and analyzed the data, he found no changes were needed in his content chapters; so he built his final outline—the one that would turn into his "Table of Contents," as shown in Figure 6.2. Here he reworded some sections to achieve grammatical parallelism in the outline. He did so for the content chapters by using appropriate connective words: *by, for, and, because,* and *although.* (To show the variations possible in using connective words, two outlines with connectives are shown in Figures 6.3 and 6.4.) The researcher now is ready to evaluate his final outline using evaluative criteria described next.

FIGURE 6.2

**Constructing and Testing an Outline
for Grammatical Parallelism**

Conditional statement: I can evaluate the plant location considerations for selected Phoenix-area manufacturers

by IV. Determining the Major Location Factors
   by Examining the Labor Supply *and*
   by Evaluating the Market Accessibility *and*
   by Investigating the Tax Structure *and*
   by Accessing Pre-Production Factors *and*
   by Identifying Secondary Factors *and*

by V. Evaluating the Attractiveness of Phoenix
   for Labor Supply *and*
   for Market Accessibility *and*
   for Tax Structure *and*
   for Land and Construction Costs *and*
   for Climate and Water Availability

   VI. Conclusions and Recommendations

With the final outline constructed, the researcher is
now ready to select an order of typographical gradations for
the outline headings in the research report.

Using Typographical Gradations

Typographical gradations in report writing consists of a system of heading styles designed to represent, in descending order of importance, the outline headings. Use of this system
eliminates the need for the A, B, C, and 1, 2, 3 designations in
the report body.

The gradation system is based upon the following premises for achieving emphasis:

1. Capital letters are more important than lower-case letters.
2. A centered heading is more important than a side heading.

3. A free-standing (above the line of writing) heading is more important than a run-in heading.
4. An underlined heading is more important than one not underlined. Upon these premises, a conventional system of typographical gradations has been established for constructing headings in the report, as shown in Figure 6.5. The purpose here is to show the system as it is often used in report-writing textbooks and manuals.

The system shown in Figure 6.5 needs to be modified for our use for two reasons:

1. Most research report style manuals and many research textbooks do not use the No. 1 degree heading style—all capitals, underlined. They show chapter titles using No. 2 degree headings.
2. Although some style manuals recommend use of degrees 4, 6, and 8 (not underlined headings), the suggestion here is that these headings *not* underlined are potential sources of reader confusion. Thus, you should not use them unless you need the extra degree of gradation for a very detailed outline.

Based upon the modifications just described, the degrees of typographical gradations will appear as shown in Figures 6.6 and 6.7. Also, the degrees shown here are now consistent with the degrees shown in the outline example in Figure 6.1.

You are free to choose any degree to represent your outline, provided the headings and degrees selected are *always* in descending order of importance consistent with the outline. Of course, if your outline requires the use of more degrees than are shown in Figures 6.6 and 6.7, then you would need to select from the system shown in Figure 6.5.

Evaluating the Outline

1. Make the captions comprehensive in wording to cover the material underneath the captions.

2. Try to have fairly equal or proportionate divisions. A three-page chapter and a fifteen-page chapter suggest infirmities in organization of material.

3. Vary the word choice and pattern in constructing headings; avoid the monotony of repetitive phrasing.

FIGURE 6.3

**Sample Outline Using Connective Words
for a Test of Parallelism**

Title: The Feasibility of Marketing LP-Gas as an Automotive Fuel in the Phoenix Area (Kenneth D. Probert. Arizona State University)

Conditional Statement: The feasibility of marketing LP-gas as an automotive fuel in Phoenix can be determined

  I.   Introduction
       Statement of the Problem
       Purpose and Need
       Scope and Limitations
       Definitions of Terms
       Review of Related Research
       Procedures
       Plan of Presentation
by II. The Characteristics of LP-Gas and Its Use in Vehicles
     by The Origin and Characteristics of LP-Gas
           for Derivation *and*
           for Physical Properties *and*
           for Vaporizing Temperatures
     by The Fuel Systems for Vehicles
           for Fuel Storage Tank *and*
           for Filter and Lock-off *and*
           for Vaporizer-Regulator *and*
           for Single- or Dual-Fuel System *and*
           for Storage Tank Location *and*
           for Safety Standards
     by The Use of LP-Gas in Engines
           for Fuel Standards *and*
           for Octane Ratings *and*
           for Maintenance Effects *and*

4. Have grammatically parallel development and phrasing.
5. Have no overlapping of topics; adhere to the principle of mutual exclusion.
6. Avoid faulty subordination, that of making a subheading equivalent to a main heading.

FIGURE 6.3 (Continued)

---

      for Engine Life *and*
      for Engine Power
by III. The LP-Gas Marketing System
   for A Profile of the Industry
      by Industry Statistics *and*
      by Relevance of Statistics
   for LP-Gas Supplies, Present and Future
      by Diversion from the Petrochemical Market *and*
      by Imported Gas
   for LP-Gas Facilities in the Phoenix Area
      by Present Engine Market *and*
      by Retail Sales at Distributorships
   for Costs of Using LP-Gas Compared with Gasoline
      by Costs of Conventional Equipment *and*
      by Fuel Costs *and*
      by Total Ownership Cost
by IV. External Factors Affecting Automotive Fuel Market
   for Shortages of Competitive Fuels
      by Extent of Shortage *and*
      by Reason for Shortage *and*
      by Possible Role of LP-Gas
   for Governmental Pollution Restrictions
      by Exhaust Gas Pollutants *and*
      by Pollution Effects of LP-Gas Versus Gasoline *and*
      by Federal Emissions Requirements *and*
      by Catalytic Converters *and*
      by Need for More Fuel
   for Retail Station Zoning Regulations
      by Zoning *and*
      by Fire Code
   V. Summary, Conclusions, and Recommendations
      Summary
      Conclusions
      Recommendations

---

7. Avoid faulty coordination, that of making a main heading equivalent to a subheading.
8. Attempt a reasonable outline length, perhaps not more than six to eight major divisions and the same for the

FIGURE 6.4

**Sample Outline Using Connective Words
for a Test of Parallelism**

Title: Guides for Management Involved with Converting to a Computerized Inventory Control System (Theo Merrill, Arizona State University)

Conditional Statement: I can develop guides for management involved with converting to a computerized inventory control system

     I. Establishing Intent
       Introduction
           Problem Statement
           Project Purpose
           Scope
           Definition of Terms
       Review of Literature
       Procedures
           Sources of Material
           Basic Assumptions
       Organization Plan
by II. Initiating the System Study
  by Establishing Responsibility *and*
  by Organizing the Inventory Control Systems Planning Unit
      and
  by Studying the System
     for Objectives and Policy *and*
     for Existing Procedures *and*
     for Quantitative Data *and*
     for Exception Processing *and*
     for Input-Output Scheduling *and*
     for Work Flow *and*
  by Describing the Working Papers

subdivisions. If you have more, you can revise so the increased length comes from subheadings.

9. Have no single main or subheading. If you do, no classification or organization is evident. You cannot divide

FIGURE 6.4 (Continued)

for Reports *and*
for Forms *and*
for Records *and*
by Determining the Effectiveness
by III. Designing the System
  by Introducing Principles and Objectives
    for Design Principles *and*
    for Design Objectives *and*
  by Describing a Computerized Inventory Control System
    by General Description *and*
    by Inventory Control Function *and*
  by Documenting the Proposed System
    by The Process Chart *and*
    by The Procedure Chart *and*
    by Miscellaneous Documents
by IV. Installing the Computerized System
  by Considering Delivery Implications *and*
  by Programming the Computer *and*
  by Filemaking *and*
  by Establishing Clerical Procedures *and*
  by Testing the System
by V. Operating the Computerized System
  by Obtaining Reliability
    by Planning a Realistic Schedule *and*
    by Adjusting to Perturbations *and*
  by Considering Accuracy of Operation *and*
  by Determining the Cost of Operation *and*
  by Evaluating Personnel Problems
by VI. Determining the Value for Management
  by Documenting Responsibility *and*
  by Programming *and*
  by Filemaking *and*
  by Preparing Clerical Procedures *and*
  by Setting Operating Procedures

FIGURE 6.5

**Principle of Typographical Gradation Showing
Possible Headings in Descending Order of Importance**

Heading Degree	Heading Style
1	All capital letters, centered, underlined
2	All capital letters, centered, *not* underlined
3	Capitals and "lowers," centered, underlined
4	Capitals and "lowers," centered, *not* underlined
5	Capitals and "lowers," side head, underlined, freestanding
6	Capitals and "lowers," side head, *not* underlined, freestanding
7	Capitals and "lowers," side head, underlined, run-in
8	Capitals and "lowers," side head, *not* underlined, run-in

something and end up with one. If you have an A, you
must have a B. If you do not, the A must become a part of
that which you were attempting to divide.
10. Make relationships apparent, such as that derived from
testing the outline using connective words: *by, for, and,
because,* and *although.*

With your final outline pointing the way, you are now
ready to begin writing the first draft of your research report.
Writing the introduction, described next in Chapter 7, consists mainly of reshaping your research proposal.

FIGURE 6.6

Recommended typographical gradations

Heading Degree	Heading Style
2	All capital letters, centered
3	Capitals and "lowers," centered, underlined
5	Capitals and "lowers," side head, underlined, freestanding
7	Capitals and "lowers," side head, underlined, run-in

FIGURE 6.7

Recommended system of typographical gradations shown as headings. The numbers correspond to the heading degrees shown in Figure 6.6.

> **Chapter III**
> **2** **The Research Design**
>
> The research design consisted of selecting methods of primary and secondary data collection, data treatment, and follow-up procedures. Other data were collected through correspondence with NASS and an interview. . . .
>
> **3** *Data Collection Methods*
>
> The sources of data for this study were both primary and secondary. The primary data were developed from a mailed questionnaire survey. Two questionnaires were mailed to selected firms. . . .
>
> **5** *Collection of Primary Data*
>
> The questionnaire was selected as the primary method of data collection for the following reasons:
>
> > 1. A wider geographical dispersion was available than would be practical by the interview method.
> > 2. The use of questionnaires in this pilot or exploratory study would test the feasibility of this method for future research. Problems encountered with these returns could be avoided in the. . . .
>
> **7** *Selection of the Firms Surveyed.* Manufacturers in the Phoenix area, as defined in the scope of this study, were selected from the *Arizona Directory of Manufacturers,* 1974, which was provided by. . . .
>
> **7** *Treatment of Data.* The questionnaires were designed to provide both quantitative and qualitative data. Quantitive data . . .

7
Writing the Introduction

This chapter contains the treatment of the introductory material in the research report; it overlaps and expands upon the content of the research proposal described in Chapter 3. The introduction is your preliminary conference with the reader; it must help your reader to zero in on your work and set the basis for your research. Discussed in this chapter are:

1. Developing a writing plan
2. Describing background material
3. Identifying the research problem and associated elements
4. Reviewing the related literature and research
5. Reporting the research procedures
6. Providing a chapter transition

Developing a Writing Plan

Many combinations of subtopics are possible for an introduction, but to provide you with a starting point the following writing plan is presented as a guide.

1. Give a short background statement to orient the reader.
2. Tell why the study is important or needs doing. Tell who needs the answers or what brought the problem about.
3. Describe what has been done before your study.
4. State the research problem. On the basis of what you just said in numbers 1, 2 and 3, a problem needs to be answered.
5. Factor the problem by listing the specific questions to be answered. If hypotheses are a part of your research, state them following your problem. The relationship should be apparent, and your readers should not have to flip pages to see how the hypotheses evolve.
6. Include the problem-associated elements, such as *scope, limitations, purpose, need, objectives,* and *definitions of terms.*
7. Review the literature and research.
8. Describe the research procedures. Describe the instruments and forms used and any validity or reliability tests made. Tell what population was studied and describe the sampling techniques.
9. Provide a transition section to the remainder of the research report.
10. Be sure to exclude all reference to research findings in this section. To tell *what* you have found in the same section in which you introduce the problem and method is illogical.

This introductory material may be set out in one, two, or three chapters or major divisions. The number of chapters you will use depends upon the depth and complexity of such features as the review of related literature and the description of your research method. Let reasonable chapter proportion be your guide. And, although the elements and their placement as described in the foregoing writing plan are typical for the research report introduction, none are legislated. You may combine or rearrange them to correspond with any unique requirements of your research project. Let logic and your concern for reader ease in reading and understanding be your guide.

Describing Background Material

Lead off in your first chapter by telling your reader what gave rise to the problem you are investigating. The content here should set the stage so your reader will logically see a problem evolving; it should provide an easy transition to the problem statement itself.

You should be especially alert to restrict the background information to a few pages—perhaps not more than three or four at the most. A detailed background section will keep your readers away from the problem statement so long that they will think you have a well-kept secret. Your readers deserve to know quickly the background information that leads to the problem.

Guard against making this background material a history of your topic. If an extensive history or description is needed, then perhaps you should include a separate chapter for these details. If you do, be sure you revise your problem statement to include a history. The researcher is usually well advised to steer clear of including such intensive background material because more often than not it turns out to be only a page filler.

Close this section with a transition statement that leads naturally to your statement of the problem section. That is, based upon what you have said here, a question needs answering. A portion of background material is included in the example in the next section.

Identifying the Research Problem and Associated Elements

Your problem may be a single question or a general question with two or more specific subquestions (you cannot have a one-question subdivision). For example:

Although it is clear that both the ABA and the AICPA now ethically permit the dual practice of law and accounting, the conditions under which the dual practice are maintained and the desirability of the dual practice are still open to question. For example, the National Conference of Lawyers and Certified Public Accountants, in a statement issued in 1970, said that it had considered the matter of dual practice for many years and is convinced that it is not in the public interest for anyone to engage in the practice of both professions.

Statement of the Problem

From the controversial issues on dual practice the problem evolves: What is the current thought of Phoenix-area lawyers and CPAs on the acceptability of the dual practice of lawyer-CPA? To answer this question, the dual-practitioner problem was factored into three sub-problems:

1. How adequately does the dual practitioner serve the public interest?
2. What is the current thought on the competence of the dual practitioner?
3. What are the conditions under which the dual practitioner may conduct himself in a professional manner?
   —Louis J. Camarella, Jr., Arizona State University

If validation of an hypothesis was an integral part of your study, then your hypothesis should be stated here along with the assumptions upon which it is based. For example:

The Problem

. . . The problem of this study was to determine the effect that fewer work-sampling days (fewer than fifteen or the work cycle) has on the sample estimate; and to determine the effect, if any, that the number of observations has on the sample estimate when the days in the study are held constant. Specifically, this study should provide a tentative answer to the question: "Can the overall time (number of days) for Acme Company work-sampling studies be reduced and still provide results that are not significantly different from lengthier studies?"

The Hypothesis

To determine both the validity and practicality of fewer sampling days (fewer than the work cycle of fifteen days) in a work sample, the following hypothesis was developed: Fewer work-sampling days provide an estimate that is not significantly different from the estimate of the original study which was developed with a greater number of days in the work sample. An underlying hypothesis, although not expressly stated, is that the sample estimate and the number of days in the sample is secondary.

Before testing this hypothesis, four assumptions needed to be made. These were: (1) the percent of the sample estimate of the original study is an accurate estimate; (2) that stability was present during the period of the study and each of the daily percentages that exceeded three sigma limits were evaluated and found to be attributable to a recurring, assignable cause; (3) that the tolerable error for all work centers that would be work-sampled is plus or minus three percent—absolute; and (4) that the Acme Company will continue to use the "lead team" concept when using the work-sampling technique to develop manpower standards.

—Arthur Jacobs, Arizona State University

Stating The Research Purpose

For some research studies, the researcher may be directed to state a purpose or objective of the study rather than to state a problem in question form. For example:

Purpose of the Study

The purpose of this study was: (1) to compare the contribution practices of the medium-size corporations with those of the larger and smaller corporations; (2) to ascertain the value of a written contribution policy to the medium-size corporation; and (3) to arrive at a basic policy that could be used with some modification by most medium-size corporations.

—Vincent Salotti, Arizona State University

Whichever method you choose, be precise with your labels. A *problem* cannot logically be a *purpose*. Yet, in many theses and dissertations these two words are used synonymously. Precision in your use of words would prohibit such indiscriminate word use. A *problem* is a question raised for inquiry, consideration, or solution. A *purpose*, however, is the reason for which something is done; the object or end to be attained. Therefore, if you use a caption containing the word *problem*, then a question is implied to be forthcoming in the content below the caption. If no question is given, then the caption would probably be a variant of "Purpose of the Study." Under this caption would be a statement of the ends to be attained or a statement of the objectives of the study.

If you choose to have both a problem statement and a purpose statement, then you will need to be sure the purpose is not merely a restatement of the problem. The purpose will, in this instance, be: "why" you are doing the study; for what reason; who can use the answer; who or what group can benefit from knowing. For example:

Purpose and Significance of the Study

The purpose of this study was to synthesize and analyze the many arguments both for and against the concurrent practice of accounting and law. What were the opinions of the members of the legal and accounting professions concerning the dual practice? What certain aspects of the dual practice did both professions agree and disagree on? What aspects of the dual practice received major support and little support?

This study was significant in measuring the degree of consensus in either profession regarding the desirability or the undesirability of the dual practice, and whether the dual practice is a problem that needs consideration in the law-and-accounting profession today. If the dual practice is desirable, undesirable, or a problem to many members of either profession, new rules of professional conduct might be developed to prohibit or restrict the dual practice in both or either professions, or a separate professional organization might be developed to govern dual practitioners. If the dual practice is not a problem to either profession, the proper approach might be to prohibit improper or unethical conduct of the lawyer-CPA on a case-by-case basis and not on an all-inclusive edict.

—Louis J. Camarella, Jr., Arizona State University

Or

Purpose of the Study

For persons interested in the airport management field as a career, a source of information on how to prepare for airport management work is needed. Thus, the purpose of this study is to provide this information in a useful way. Few training courses are available that provide the necessary high-quality background, but it may be possible to develop a study program that would be available at many educational institutions. If such a program is inadequate, it may be necessary to develop a program of independent study.

    —Robert W. Hutchins, Arizona State University

Many combinations of the elements described in this section are available to you. The criteria governing your choice should be precision and reader understanding.

Describing Scope and Limitations

The *scope* defines the boundaries you place on your problem, and the *limitations* explain the restrictions or handicaps affecting your study. Whether you choose to have a separate section with the caption "Scope and Limitations" (or variants of this caption) or to describe the problem boundaries in the "Statement of the Problem" section is immaterial. A review of theses and dissertations completed show predominant use of the separate "Scope and Limitations" or variants captions. An examination of the usual content under this caption, however, will show that many researchers do not distinguish *between* scope and limitations. Often a reader cannot determine what is actually scope and what is a limitation, or where one leaves off and the other begins.

Start this section with an explanation of the confines of your problem. The once popular reference to "delimiting the problem" is the same as describing the problem's scope. You may confine your study: (1) to a segment of a universe, (2) to a particular geographical area, (3) to a time period, (4) to selected features, such as social, political, legal, or economic,

(5) to selected characteristics or criteria, or (6) to combinations of the foregoing. You may even find it appropriate to tell what aspect of the problem you are *not* covering—and why. And, your avoidance of the word "limited to" in describing the study scope will help to assure accuracy when you set out the study limitations next. The "Scope" section is the spot to draw a tight circle around your problem. For example:

Scope of the Study

Examined in this study are the variety of related decisions that go to make up the distinct inventory control system. What happens to this system and what should happen under the guise of responsible management, during installation and operation of a computerized inventory approach, is of primary interest.

Inventory control involves the functions of calculating economic order quantities, reorder points, buffer stocks, and normal procedures of recording inventory transactions. The mathematical or quantitative aspects of these functions, however, are excluded. Attention instead is directed toward the functions necessary for installation and operation of the system in an organizational sense.

Further, not covered in this study is the technical portion of conversion, for management is usually well provided with programming instructions, computer routines, and guidance on physical installation and design. Thus, any analysis of the physical computer or the organizational unit responsible for operating it (programmers, machine operators) will be done only to illustrate the procedure management is concerned with during installation and operation of the electronic inventory control system.

—Theo Merrill, Arizona State University

Describe the study limitations in terms of the restrictions or handicaps placed upon you. Typical restrictions you face are lack of time, money, and access to certain data, subjective data, and the like. In no instance, however, should a lack of ability (or knowledge) excuse poor performance in doing a study. If you believe you lack such ability, then by all means you have selected the wrong problem to investigate. Here is a sample "Limitations" section:

Limitations

Any mail survey has inherent limitations. Seldom is it possible to ask enough questions in the questionnaire to cover all aspects of a given subject, or to obtain replies from all of the individuals contacted. The use of the questionnaire can also cause biased or incorrect results if an unknowledgable person in the firm fills in the answers. Still another limitation may be that planning is a somewhat nebulous subject to many businessmen, and because of this factor it is sometimes difficult to evaluate the real meaning of the respondent's answers.

Personal or even telephone interviews would have permitted reading between the lines, as it were, and obtaining more in-depth information than through the use of a mail questionnaire. But, because of the geographical boundaries chosen for this study, it was impractical from both a time and financial standpoint to conduct interviews.

A further limiting factor, aside from time and finances, is the lack of research studies and other current literature on the subject of long-range planning for financial institutions. Fortunately, several studies have been completed on long-range planning practices in other industries. These studies helped to establish the necessary criteria for evaluating the savings and loan associations' long-range planning practices.

—P. Edwin Rife, Arizona State University

Defining the Terms

The primary purpose of the "Definitions of Terms" section is to specify the precise meaning intended for words or terms subject to different interpretations. A secondary purpose for this section may be to serve as a reader convenience to save the effort of referring to a dictionary. One should assume, however, that the reader has at least a general or working knowledge of the subject being researched. This assumption should help to assure a judicious selection of terms is included.

You have four choices for placing definitions in your report: (1) insert as a subdivision in the "Introduction" chapter; (2) define, in apposition, the first time the term is used in any narrative portion of the report; (3) include as a glossary of terms in the "Appendix"; or (4) use combinations of the foregoing choices. Whichever method you choose, consider the practicality of alphabetizing the list and making the entries grammatically consistent. Emphasize the term defined by underlining or by using some other emphasis device (placement or type face) to be sure your reader will catch the entry quickly and easily.

Define the terms by using a dictionary (general or specialized), by citing an authority in the field, or by calling on your experience. If the definition is not your construction, be sure to cite the authority or source.

You can define the term by identifying the *class* (genus) to which the *term* (species) belongs and then by *differentiating* that species from other members of that class, as shown in Figure 7.1.

Thus, in defining "condominium" you can first identify the genus "dwelling" and then note how it differs from other types of dwellings in such elements as construction, style, and function. See Figure 7.2.

General suggestions for constructing definitions are:

1. Use words that are likely to be more familiar to your reader than the term being defined.
2. The term defined should not be a part of the definition.

FIGURE 7.1

Relationship of *species*, *class*, and *differentia* in constructing a definition

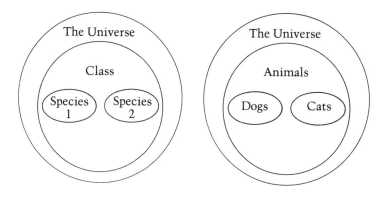

FIGURE 7.2

Application of *species* to a specific item—Condominium A.

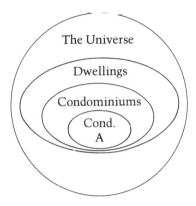

3. Try not to use abstract or vague words to define a term.
4. If you need to amplify a definition for clarity, use these means:

analogy   example
exclusion   physical description
effects   comparison or contrast

Just remember, the basic purpose for defining terms is to let your reader know how *you* are using the terms in this research project. Here are some examples:

Definitions of Terms

Forecast.—An estimate of the future value of a parameter, such as demand, based upon prior observation of the parameter. A "forecast" is to be differentiated from a "prediction." Observation over nine periods resulting in the series 2, 2, 2, 2, 2, 2, 2, 2, and 2 would lead one to forecast that the value in the tenth period will also be 2.

Inventory policy.—A rule, expressed in mathematical equations and logic, which specifies one or more of the following parameters for management of an inventory: (1) desired quantity of each part number to be maintained in an inventory, (2) when to order replenishment stock for the inventory, and (3) how much replenishment stock to order for the inventory.

Stochastic model.—A model in which calculations of the probability that a future value will lie between two specified limits is possible.

—Arthur J. Hallinan, Jr., Arizona State University

Reviewing the Related Literature and Research

The main purpose of the literature review is to identify a void in existing knowledge. This void, when identified, will show how your efforts can help to complete some total picture. You should not usually perceive yourself as a lone pioneer in some problem area. More likely your research will fit into a broader scheme of research results.

Secondary purposes for the literature review are: (1) to contribute ideas for the research design; (2) to furnish evaluative techniques or criteria; (3) to provide opinions or perspective about your problem area; and (4) to identify findings that will support or contrast with your findings.

A common misconception is that the purpose of the review is to provide an annotated bibliography of researches somewhat related to the one under way, or to show that the research being attempted has not already been done by someone else. Both are only incidental outcomes from a literature review.

The content volume for this section will determine whether you incorporate it with the introductory chapter or relegate it to a separate chapter. For a study that has a dearth of related literature or research, or both, the review could easily be included in Chapter 1 content without making the chapter disproportionate in length to the remaining chapters. For an extensive review, you may elect to place it in a separate chapter, usually Chapter 2. Whether it is made a separate chapter or a part of Chapter 1, place the review *ahead of* the "Procedures" chapter or section. Because the research design or methods may stem in part from the review of literature, logic would make the procedures section *follow* the review.

Basic organization for this section may be by (1) related literature, and (2) related research—dependent upon the volume for

each, of course. The organization for each may be further classified by: (1) time sequence; (2) categories (functions, criteria,
events); or by (3) decreasing relationship or importance to your
study. If you treat the literature and research review as one, then
organize the chapter on one of the three bases just mentioned.

The two examples following are the introductions to related literature chapters. These excerpts show how this chapter content may be organized.

CHAPTER 1

Review of Current Literature

Ideas and techniques of long-range planning are summarized in
this chapter. The writings of Hastings, Buchele, and Haas com-
prise most of the ideas reviewed, but other writings from periodicals and S.B.A. publications are included as they appeared
pertinent. The chapter includes sections on (1) formulation of
objectives, (2) forecasting, and (3) actual planning of activities.
These three areas are each a vital part of long-range planning
and are inseparably linked, as is pointed out in this chapter.

—Carl G. King, Arizona State University

CHAPTER 2

Related Literature and Research

Many articles and books have been written about the nature
and use of suggestion systems. These publications generally relate favorable impressions toward suggestion systems regardless of the possible incongruities in system administration.

Presented in this chapter is the background information related to the problem through a discussion of the history of suggestion systems, the evolution of the National Association of
Suggestion Systems, and various current viewpoints toward
system features and administration, all of which help to point
to how this present research fits into the overall picture.

—George F. Aulbach, Jr., Arizona State University

Even if the data for your study come entirely from secondary sources (such as for an historical study or a synthesis

and analysis of current literature), you still need to include a separate section of *related research* somewhere in the introductory material. The following example (a condensed version) will point the way for presenting related research.

Review of Related Research

Much has been written on the subject of sensitivity training over the last fifteen years, but very little empirical data relates sensitivity training to organizational effectiveness. Foreman (1985) conducted a study on the current thought on sensitivity training, and this present study is an attempt to expand on his study.

Several research studies relate to peripheral areas of sensitivity training. Hand, Richards, and Slocum (1983) studied the organizational climate necessary for a human relations program. Golembiewski (1980) tested various models of attitudinal change, and Ivancevich (1984) made a detailed study of trainer styles and group development. All of these studies appeared to be methodologically sound; however, they did not relate directly to the effects of sensitivity training.

Other studies have been conducted on sensitivity training as it has been applied to organizations. Argyris (1982) found an increase in listening ability, patience, trust, mutual confidence, and openness after sensitivity training. Boyd and Elliss (1982) found many positive effects from sensitivity training but could not link them to organizational effectiveness. De Michele (1986) found opposite results from sensitivity training to what most other researchers have found. Hand and Slocum (1980) discovered a greater awareness of self and others; however, this effect was negated after three months. Gilligan (1984) found an increase in self-reliance and support after a twenty-four-hour training session. Wohlking (1980) also found positive effects from sensitivity training but recommended drastic changes to organizational structure and procedures in order to accommodate the changed behavior.

Many other research studies and articles have been written on nearly all facets of sensitivity training. Very few of them, however, have attempted to link sensitivity training to organizational effectiveness; and most of them are anecdotal and subjective.

—Larry G. Christensen, Arizona State University

Reporting the Research Procedures

Describe in this section how you went about solving your problem. Relate the procedures, step-by-step, in enough detail so another researcher could redo your study and likely achieve similar results. Your procedures, of course, are based on your research design; therefore, describe and justify how your study was set up. Include, as appropriate, such items as:

- method, basis, and size for sample selection
- questionnaire construction, testing, mailing, and follow-up
- tests, scales, criteria development
- statistical techniques, levels of confidence accepted
- experiment design, procedures, variables, and controls
- indexes consulted, major information sources
- procedures for testing hypotheses

As before, the volume of the content for describing research procedures will determine whether you make this section a part of Chapter 1 or a separate chapter. Note for your chapter title, though, a *procedure* is defined as being a *method* or a *process.* Therefore, title this section or chapter "Research Procedures" or "Research Methods" (or variants) but not the redundant "Methods and Procedures." And, why not lay to rest the rather pompous term "methodology" as a chapter title.

Because of the importance of research procedures in setting out your research design, the following procedures description from a student's pilot study is included in its entirety. This description is presented only to show the type of content, not necessarily a model research design.

CHAPTER 3
The Research Procedures

The primary source of data for this study was a mail questionnaire survey. Two questionnaires were mailed to selected firms to determine the extent that suggestion systems are being used in the Phoenix area, how successful these systems are, and what features are common to the more successful systems. It was anticipated that returned questionnaires would verify the hypotheses that suggestion systems are not widely used by manufacturing firms; that success of the systems in use differs; and that the more successful systems have particular ingredients essential to their success.

Secondary sources of data relating background information and current viewpoints were provided by books and articles located in the Hayden Library. Arizona State University. The *Abridged Reader's Guide to Periodical Literature* and *Business Periodicals Index* were consulted along with the library card catalogue to point out available literature. These sources provided an investigative departure point for preparation of the questionnaires.

Other information was obtained through correspondence with NASS and an interview with the Suggestion System Administrator of one of the largest local manufacturing firms. NASS provided a list of their available publications along with a statistical report and several other pieces of literature. The personal interview gave an insight into the problems of operating a successful suggestion system.

The Research Design

The research design for this pilot study involved selecting methods of data collection, data treatment, and follow-up procedures.

Questionnaire Method.—The questionnaire was selected as the primary method of data collection for the following reasons:

1. A wider geographical dispersion was available than would be practicable by the interview method.
2. The use of questionnaires in this pilot study would test the feasibility of this method for future research. Problems encountered with these returns could be avoided in the future project.

Selection of Firms Surveyed.—Manufacturers of the Phoenix area, as defined in the scope of this study, were selected from the *Arizona Directory of Manufacturers,* which was provided by the Phoenix Chamber of Commerce. This directory lists approximately 700 manufacturers in the Phoenix metropolitan area, of which 117 have fifty or more employees. All of the firms with fifty or more employees were considered in this survey. The conclusions drawn are aimed only at this particular universe.

This size firm was selected for two reasons. First, it was necessary to narrow the scope of the investigation to be commensurate with the available time. Second, related literature indicated that very small firms normally do not operate suggestion systems because of the close working relationship between employer and employees. This latter fact was also verified by Evan W. LaRue in his unpublished Master's thesis, "Survey of Current Practices by California Manufacturers Concerning Suggestion Systems" 1965, Arizona State University. Mr. LaRue's survey revealed that 38 percent of the manufacturers in California with more than one thousand employees had suggestion systems. Indications were apparent that the smaller the firm is, fewer suggestion systems exist. Therefore, surveying the 583 firms with fewer than fifty employees in this area would contribute little, if any, value to this study.

Treatment of Data.—The questionnaires were designed to provide both quantitative and qualitative data. Quantitative data revealed the extent that suggestion systems are used by manufacturers in the Phoenix area and indicated features common to these systems. Qualitative data revealed attitudes and motives contributing to the extent that systems are used. Quantitative data are illustrated and qualitative data are discussed in Chapter IV.

Criteria for determining the more successful suggestion systems were established. These criteria were: (1) employee participation by percent; (2) the tangible and intangible benefits being derived by both employer and employee: (3) attitudes toward the system; and (4) system performance in relation to the system objectives. The more successful systems were identified for future detailed investigation.

Follow-up Procedures.—The questionnaire returns indicated a need for personal follow-up in several areas. Because time was a factor, however, the follow-up action was deleted from the research plan of this pilot study. Revisions of the questionnaires will minimize follow-up needs in the future research.

Preparation of the Questionnaires

Because of the limited time established by externally imposed deadlines, the questionnaires were not tested in the manufacturing industry prior to mailing. The initial drafts were, however, critiqued by two College of Business faculty members before the final draft was reproduced and mailed.

Two different questionnaires were prepared. One was designed for responding firms that are not operating a suggestion system; and the other was designed to collect detailed information from firms with a system.

The first questionnaire was prepared to establish the percentage of firms that do not have suggestion systems and to indicate attitudes of these firms toward suggestion systems. This information is desirable for possible future investigation. A copy of this questionnaire appears in Appendix B.

The second questionnaire was to be completed only by firms operating some form of suggestion system. This questionnaire was designed to gather quantitative data concerning system features along with qualitative data expressing opinions and attitudes as illustrated in Appendix C.

Each questionnaire is a combination of the closed-form and free-form type. The respondents were asked to make a choice among alternatives in most questions, while other questions called for a free response with no clues provided.

The questionnaires were mailed on Friday, November 11, 198x, so that they would likely be received by the respondents on Monday, thereby avoiding the weekend in-basket pileup.

All questionnaires were addressed to the company president by name or to the general manager if the president was unknown. *The Arizona Directory of Manufacturers* provided the name of the company president in most instances.

The Cover Letter

The cover letter was written to induce the respondent to participate in a survey; therefore, the opening words made clear what was wanted and why. The letter was intended to be straightforward and appealing. Detailed instructions were related pertaining to the questionnaires, and a return addressed envelope was enclosed. The respondents were promised that the name of their firm would be held in confidence. A copy of the cover letter is shown in Appendix A.

Questionnaire Returns

The survey included all manufacturing firms in the Phoenix area with fifty or more employees. This population includes

117 firms, of which 51 responded to the questionnaires. The respondents comprised 43.5 percent of the population; however, four responses were not usable because of lack of information or identification. The usable returns comprised 40 percent of the population. The returned questionnaires are being retained and are available only through the author of this study. Tabulation of the answers is contained in Appendix D.

Statistical Validity

No attempt was made to draw any statistical inferences from this pilot study. Statistical treatment will be necessary, however, for firm and specific conclusions in the future research project.

    —George F. Aulbach, Jr., Arizona State University

Providing a Chapter Transition

This section of your research report is known as the "Organization Plan" or "Plan of Presentation," and it furnishes the transition needed for your reader to move to Chapter 2. It is a brief look at how the remainder of your presentation unfolds. The purpose of this section differs from the purpose of the "Table of Contents" in that the contents page provides a *listing* of content, whereas this section contains a description of "what," "where," and "why." Also, a quick recap at this point of the major elements you are covering helps to bridge the gap for your reader. The following is an example:

Organizational Plan

Contributions in several areas are integrated and extended to answer the question: "How can a manufacturer establish inventory levels for his service centers?" This problem is related to inventory control and provisioning. The literature of these areas is therefore reviewed in Chapter 2.

    The nature of an inventory, including service-parts inventories, is to be responsive to demand. But demand is a future and, hence, unknown value at the time inventory levels must be established. The manufacturer must have adequate service-part inventories to achieve some level of customer satisfaction. Yet, having too much stock will result in inventory write-offs as service parts become obsolete. The problem of treating the service-part life cycle is therefore addressed in Chapter 3 to set the stage for Chapters 4 and 5.

A key to solution of the problem lies with the manufacturer's ability to assess future values of demand rate. Two approaches are available—forecasting and prediction. Forecasting techniques are considered in Chapter 4; prediction techniques are covered in Chapter 5.

With the expected future defined by the manufacturer, it is then possible to optimize his service-part inventory decisions. This optimization is discussed in Chapter 6. Limitations of the study preclude development of an actual optimization technique but several ways to do so are presented.

Summary, conclusions, and recommendations follow in Chapter 7.

—Arthur J. Hallinan, Jr., Arizona State University

The organizational plan can be important because you may want to give a reason why you choose to present some element as you do, especially if your reader will see an alternative. This presentation will keep your readers in step with you. Especially beware of including trivia here. A statement such as, "Graphs and tables have been included for reader convenience," merely questions your readers' intelligence and wastes their time.

As a final point for writing the introduction, be sure no evidence of your study findings is included. To do so would be illogical because at this point you are describing only what you did to set up the research. Research findings belong only in the content chapters, as discussed in the next chapter.

8
Writing the Content Chapters

The content chapters contain the data and analysis that lead to the answer to the research problem or fulfill the purpose set out in the introductory chapter. Here is where the hypotheses are tested through analysis of the data, or an answer is developed through a reasoning process, or both. As such, these chapters are the heart of a research report. The approach to writing these chapters involves:

1. Reflecting the study organization
2. Previewing the chapter
3. Analyzing the data
4. Presenting the analysis
5. Summarizing the chapter

Reflecting the Study Organization

The tentative outline you constructed as described in chapter 6 provides the basis for organizing the content chapters. Here, too, is pointed up your research design. It is easy to see, then, no matter how good a job you have done in conducting the research, you can hide its merit completely with poor organization. Unfortunately, the converse is not true; that is, a good job in organization and writing cannot hide a poor job in research. Experience shows that many research reports are misleading, not because of their content but because of the way they are structured.

Even at this point in organizing the content chapters you should not consider your outline as final. You still will want to be open for suggestions and revisions as you write the analysis. Adding, deleting, and revising headings can be expected up to the final-draft stage.

Important next is planning the sequence of content for each segment of the outline. How will you present your interpretation of the facts in a logical fashion to your reader? The underlying thought here is to make it as easy as possible for the reader to get the information out of the report—not how easy will it be for you to get the information in between the report covers. A strategy for writing the content chapters can best be shown graphically as in Figure 8.1.

Previewing the Chapter

Start each content chapter with a description of how the chapter is to contribute to answering the problem, the methods used for this portion of the study, and what points are covered. Use these guides:

1. State the chapter objectives, or relationships to previous chapters, or both.
2. Describe any special procedures used in the chapter.
3. Name the major subdivisions in their sequence.

Writing an introduction or preview requires a rare skill: that skill is the ability to provide the essentials quickly and

FIGURE 8.1

Strategy for Writing a Content Chapter

Content Chapter Title

Chapter preview

Subheading 1

Generalization of overall answer for this section A topic sentence lead
Data and analysis, verbal and statistical—tables, charts, graphs
Summary in words different from the opening section

Subheading 2

Generalization of overall answer for this section A topic sentence lead
Data and analysis, verbal and statistical—tables, charts, graphs
A summarization in words different from the opening section

Subheading 3

Generalization of overall answer for this section A topic sentence lead
Data and analysis, verbal and statistical—tables, charts, graphs
Summary in words different from the opening section

Chapter Summary

Resolve the foregoing subanswers to a subconclusion for this chapter. It should answer a subquestion from Chapter 1 and show a contribution to answering the overall research problem.

completely. If you say too much, you will cause a reader to skim the material; say too little and you imply inability, aloofness, or disinterest. Following are examples of suggested approaches to the chapter preview.

> The historical manner of conducting labor-management negotiations in the copper mining industry has been one of plant-by-plant, company-by-company negotiations. The unions have long sought to end this system, but union strife and company resistance have combined to retain the *status quo*.
>
> In this chapter, the effects of the merger of the Mine, Mill and Smelter Workers Union with the United Steelworkers Union upon contract negotiations are studied. The list of unions collaborating are described and their contract offers as published are discussed. Finally, a compilation of the six-month history of contract negotiations is evaluated.
> —Robert Kemp, Arizona State University

Or, include a transitional statement to relate this chapter to the previous chapter:

> This chapter contains an explanation of the statistical results obtained using the methods described in Chapter 3. An analysis of the results provides answers to the questions posed in Chapter 1 concerning the degree and nature of the relationship between certain variables and time deposits two, four, and twelve weeks hence. Implications of the findings for bank money managers, Federal Reserve authorities, and banking theoreticians are presented throughout the chapter; and results are compared and contrasted with those uncovered in the related research and literature analyzed in Chapter 2.
> This chapter is organized into four parts. First, the degree of statistical relationship between each of the fifteen potential lead indicators and future time deposits is examined. Second, the nature of the significant relationships is investigated by examining: (a) the generality of the indicators, (b) the effect of using various lead periods, and (c) the relative importance of significant indicators. Third, statistical reliability of results is investigated by examining residuals for possible autocorrelation. Fourth, implications of the findings for bank management and theory are explained.
> —Harry Jones, Arizona State University

The chapter preview, at the very least, should alert the readers to the objective for the chapter. To omit the chapter preview is to send the readers down your road of analysis without a road map and let them make of it what they will.

Analyzing the Data

Here you have the task of revealing by reasoning the meaning of the facts you have collected and of coming to conclusions about them. Such is the process of interpretation. The research report should contain an impartial presentation of the facts based on a critical, exhaustive, and studious inquiry. This approach is more academic than practical, however, since no one is likely to be *completely* impartial. The person making an analysis should: (1) have a knowledge of the field, (2) have good judgment, (3) be honest in evaluating, and (4) be free from bias or prejudice. Yet, as those who serve on a jury sometimes find, people can hear and see the same evidence but arrive at different answers. So it sometimes is in data analysis in research.

Normally, reports are written using elements of style to increase attractiveness and readability. Sometimes, however, these elements may override for the reader the quality of the interpretation. Therefore, you should take special care in developing the logic of presentation and conclusions through interpreting the facts for the research report.

The Interpretation Process

Inherent in the interpretation process are two distinct steps. The first step is that of recognizing your attitude toward the problem with which you are dealing and toward its solution—your preliminary conclusion or theory about the meaning of the facts. And the meaning you will give to facts will depend upon such factors as your experience and knowledge in the field, your age, and your cultural background. A researcher's attitude toward interpretation should always be impartial—never with an intent to persuade or to arrive at a hoped-for answer. The best one can do, though, is to present the meaning of the facts as one sees it.

The second step in interpretation is your reasoning about the facts. Reasoning is simply a process of arriving at sound conclusions through using inferences and deductions. This use, in turn, includes considering all sides of an argument or investigation. Though it may seem only logical that this kind of thinking would be reflected in a research report, many an investigation has been made in which sound reasoning was left out completely or at least slighted considerably. This omission is unfortunate, for it is in the research project that valid reasoning is perhaps the prime requisite to an adequate conclusion.

Interpretation by Reasoning

Several techniques are used in reasoning that contribute to reader acceptance of the conclusions. One of these techniques is the use of *logic*. Connection of the various facts and events, developed during research, into a logical order can lead to the conclusions along a rational reasoning path.

A companion to the logic technique is the use of *inference*; that is, making statements about the unknown based on the known. We can make an inference about the speed of a car involved in an accident by noting its skid marks, the road conditions, and other pertinent facts. When we compare these facts to what we know to be true about skid marks, road conditions, and the like, we can make an inference about the speed of the car. Inference can be present, yet lack the quality necessary for valid judgments because the inference is illogical. You would be defeating your purpose to recognize a problem, yet reflect bias by coming to a predetermined conclusion in solving the problem. For example, the widely reported "fact" that many welfare recipients were eating canned dog food turned out to be an illogical inference. The observation of large numbers of empty dog food cans in certain neighborhoods led to the inference that the poor and welfare recipients were reduced to eating dog food. Follow-up investigation of these reports provided no basis in fact.

Analogy or correlation, through sound reasoning, can lead to a solution to a problem: but used improperly, the results of the research could be as unsatisfactory as the illogical inference just mentioned. Basically, analogy illustrates rather than proves.

Analogy is the arrangement of facts so that a new truth may be inferred. It is based on the notion that things that resemble each other in many respects resemble each other in all essential respects. For example, if a no-fault insurance plan has succeeded in New Jersey, one may assume it will succeed in Arizona. This generalization is still an assumption, though. You can relate almost any *set* of figures or circumstances to another—if you try long enough. Further, the degree of variances in many studies can be very small. Although small deviations or variations could be grounds for valid conclusions, a more careful review of the solution may show some prejudice in some of the statistics used. Proper analogy, with proper consideration to all facts, can lead to adequate solutions or areas that merit more investigation.

Generalizing is a short-cut method leading to a conclusion. The researcher concludes about all members or objects of a class based on a comparatively small number of examples. The key here is whether the sample observed is a fair proportion of the total population. And, what constitutes an adequate sample depends upon the range of differences found in the population. Basically, generalizations may be tested as follows:

1. Is the observed class too small to justify a statement about the whole class?
2. Are the examples fair examples of the whole class to which they belong?
3. Are the number of exceptions enough to cast doubt on the truth of the generalization?
4. Are the generalizations consistent with other known facts?

Assumptions are also methods of reasoning that can and do lead to valid conclusions. By assuming certain conditions, you say, in effect, that you do not have the information available, but you believe that it probably would be the way you assume. Too often, however, this means of "taking for granted" has been misused and has resulted in unsatisfactory conclusions. Assumptions can be useful tools for filling in information on questionable or unknown areas, but they can also be used as a method of plugging in information which, if the subject were to be more carefully analyzed or investigated, is in reality available. If the data are available through more intensive investigation, you would weaken the investigation by inserting your assumptions in these areas.

Using Care with Facts

Precision and depth in showing how the facts relate to the problem are important in research. Therefore, you should distinguish among and identify facts, inferences, opinions, and assumptions; the reader needs to know when you are shuttling among them. Facts are true and verifiable; they are not open to question. Thus, when someone speaks of the "true facts," that person apparently has not distinguished between facts and opinions or assumptions.

An assumption, an inference, or an opinion might be questioned because it is not reasonable under the circumstances; a fact may not. The acceptability of an assumption, for example, is related to the quality of the reasons for making the assumption.

Without analysis and reasoning, then, you would have no real research. Research is dependent upon the elements with which reasoning is concerned. It reveals the meaning of facts through a refined technique of thinking. Facts have no meaning in themselves: they acquire meaning only through interpretation. And if *you* do not interpret, you force your reader to do so.

Observing Interpretation Aids

In addition to using the factors involved in the reasoning process, you can give meaning to facts by:

- pointing out effects or consequences
- giving implications
- determining relationships
- noting similarities and differences

- identifying trends
- determining merits or faults
- making generalizations
- noting causes and effects
- determining functions
- pointing out the significance of facts
- noting recurrences or the lack of them
- evolving descriptive concepts
- proposing theories

Ask yourself questions about the data:

- How do these findings compare with related research or literature mentioned previously?
- Why is this feature significant?
- What benefits are involved? Who will benefit?
- What trends are evident? What effect might these trends have?
- How are these facts, events, or features related? What correlations exist between or among these features?
- What values can be identified—economic, social, political?
- What generalization can be made about the statistical spectrum other than the central tendency, the average?
- What is the effect of accepting or rejecting the hypothesis?
- What is the relationship to the study objective?

Unless you carry forward the data through the interpretation process and on to your conclusion, you will have presented only pages of undigested facts.

Presenting the Analysis

Features of good writing—charity, coherence, and conciseness—apply to all parts of the research report. For presenting the data analysis, however, two elements of writing style, *person* and *tense*, need review and comment. Also, because graphics and tables aid in writing presentation, these devices are discussed in this section.

Recognizing Style

Conventional practice in writing formal research reports is to use impersonal style. That is, no first- or second-person pronouns (e.g., I, me, my, we, our, us, you, or your) are used. This style may lead writers to use sometimes confusing references to themselves such as, "The author believes . . ." or "The investigator noted . . ." Restructuring the sentence to eliminate such references would lead to, "The belief here is . . ." or "As noted in this investigation . . ." The point to remember is that *you* are doing the verbalizing in the report; so unless otherwise noted, these are your thoughts being presented. Too, distinguish carefully between the terms *impersonal* style and *objective* style. Impersonal style, as noted, concerns pronoun reference, a practice that tends to put the emphasis on the facts being presented rather than on the writer. Objective style, though, excludes emotion and feeling; it stresses the factual and observable. The objective style excludes "value judgments" or emotional descriptors such as *attractive, beautiful, modest, reasonable, negligent.* Thus, writing in objective style deemphasizes the use of inferences and judgments, but since both inferences and judgments are required in the analysis, we are not likely to be *completely* objective in writing a research report.

What tense to use in presenting the analysis is sometimes a point of contention. Some believe the research report should be written primarily in past tense, because the researcher is telling what has been done. Present and future tenses may be used, of course, provided the basis for the shift is made clear to the reader. Perhaps more support is generated for writing in a present-time viewpoint, focusing on the continued existence of the presentation. The facts you generated not only were true yesterday, but also are true today. So, the emphasis in writing is on currentness and timeliness. Such is the point of view supported in this text. When definite shifts are required to past or future events, then those tenses are used. Thus, one would write in present-time viewpoint such as:

present	Chapter 4, next, contains the data and analysis for testing the hypothesis.
past and present	Only nineteen percent of those who answered the questionnaire favor the new plan.
present	Jones, writing in the *Personnel Journal*, suggests that Transactional Analysis is overrated.
past	Questionnaires were mailed to 130 suppliers.
present and future	These data suggest few banks will be willing to participate in such a venture.

The following excerpts from two research projects reflect the principles just described. The use of a topic sentence to start the content sections gives an overall generalization to your reader quickly. With this generalization, your reader can be in step with you as you describe your analysis. For example:

> A great range of prices is noted for each hospital commodity surveyed as is shown in Table IV. Just what accounts for this great range is a matter for speculation. Quantity discounts is at least one rather obvious reason for the price range. The larger the hospital, the lower the prices is evident in Table IV. A larger hospital would presumably use relatively larger quantities of all items, although exceptions are noted to this generalization. Still, this theory of quantity discount does not account for the wide range within a hospital size group or the overlapping encountered on several commodity prices. Especially noted is item 13, salt; within the medium-size hospital group, prices ranged from $17.00 to $37.50.
> —Don Ayres, Arizona State University

Or,

Noting Factors That Influence Housing Costs

The price of a typical home is increasing faster than the average family's income. The cost of maintenance, utilities, and repairs is increasing; land prices and construction material costs are rising. For more and more middle-class families, the goal of owning a new home seems to be more difficult to attain.

Housing starts have been decreasing for over a year, although the potential demand is high. A surplus of unsold homes exists because completion rates are ahead of sales. Many homes put under construction months ago are coming on the market at a time when fewer people are ready and willing to buy. If it were not for this surplus, new-home prices would be even higher.

The massive business failures and unemployment taking place in the building industry and among manufacturers and suppliers of home products also translate into higher priced shelter. After a layoff, mobilizing again for production costs money, and these costs get passed on to home buyers and renters.

Inflation has driven up housing costs rapidly over the last five years, as is shown in Figure 1, page 26. The typical new house in 1974 ran about $38,600 compared with $27,900 in 1969—a jump of nearly 40 percent. In many areas of the country, particularly major cities or in nearby suburbs, increases are even higher. According to a recent study by the Congressional Joint Economic Committee, a typical split-level house in suburbia now costs $41,300 new or $35,600 used, and only families with incomes upward of $23,000 can afford to buy them. [Actual footnotes are excluded from this example.] Hence, the average price on a single-family house rose about 21 percent in the past two years.[2] Also, land costs have risen inexorably in most places. The cost has doubled over the last three years, approximately one-third a year. . . .[3]

The cost of a new house is likely to climb faster than the general cost of living, making it difficult for middle-class Americans to move into a new home. Today, the problem is not only one of housing the nation's poor, but housing the middle class.

The trend in 1975 will be toward smaller homes with fewer built-in conveniences, and with lower price tags. The size of the average new single-family house is expected to shrink from 1,600 square feet in 1974 to 1,450 in 1975.[8] As a result, many American families have been 'priced out' of their housing dreams. Instead, the forced march is toward townhouses, cluster housing, multiplexes, condominium apartments, and the 'no frills' single-family house.

  —Shirley D. Heller, Arizona State University

Using Tabular and Graphic Devices

Tabular and graphic language is an important part of the written analysis. Both are important because some parts of the reasoning process lend themselves better to tabular-graphic-verbal discussion than to verbal discussion alone.

In practical use in the research report, tables should be separated as a class from graphics. A *table* is defined as a display of related facts, figures, or values, in an orderly sequence, in rows and columns, with either boxed or unboxed constructions. So, a table is always captioned "table." You should use a table when you want: (1) to show relationships that are not easily or readily discernible in the raw data, and (2) to facilitate the presentation of facts to help the reader. When the relationship or presentation of only two items is involved, a table is, of course, of little use.

Use the following checklist to evaluate a table:

1. Could the table stand alone if it were removed from the report? Is it independent, with all elements identified?
2. Are the data closely related? Is it a logical unit?
3. Have you used a comprehensive, clear, concise, and accurate title? A table is a list of something, and the title should name that of which the title is a list.
4. Are all units specified and sources acknowledged?
5. Have you captioned all columns?
6. Does the table facilitate your analysis and the written presentation?

Graphics may be referred to as picturization; that is, graphics are vehicles for presenting ideas, facts, or statistics through meaningful pictorial symbols. These symbols consist mainly of the bar, the line, and the pie (circle), used for presenting statistical data; and mainly pictorial maps, organization charts, diagrams, and flow charts used for presenting non-statistical facts and ideas. Unlike tables, graphics may be captioned by either of two general methods: (1) "exhibit," "illustration," or "figure," or (2) by the graphic's actual name if several of that type are used, such as "Graph 1, 2, 3, 4, 5" or "Chart 1, 2, 3, 4, 5" or "Map 1, 2, 3, 4, 5."

In general, select graphics to present the following:

to show	use
trend and movement of continuous data; growth or change over a time period	line charts
gradual, regular movements, or change	band, belt, and surface charts
sizes or amounts at different times; relative size or amount of several things at the same time; comparisons	bar charts (vertical or horizontal) and pictographs
steps or stages of a process or plan	flow chart or organization chart
geographical or spatial distribution	map chart
abstractions, circuits, mechanical devices, principles, relationships, visualizations	drawings, diagrams, photographs

Use the following checklist to evaluate graphics:

1. Could the graphic stand alone if it were removed from the report? Are all elements identified?
2. Are all units or increments specified and all sources acknowledged?
3. Have you used a comprehensive, clear, concise, and accurate title?
4. Are all lines, scales, and variables identified?
5. Has a key been included to identify lines, shadings, or colors?
6. If the report containing the graphics is to be reproduced in black and white, have colors been excluded for identifying variables?
7. Does the graphic facilitate your presentation?

The researcher's primary task in analysis is to determine what the data mean, and that task extends to interpretation of the data presented in the tables and graphics. As with a verbal presentation, tables and graphics have no meaning in themselves. They acquire meaning only in terms of a reader's interpretation, which may be entirely different from what you intend to convey: or they may acquire no meaning at all if the reader lacks the experience or ability to interpret. Thus, you must tell in your words what you want the reader to see in the table or graphic. Help the reader by pointing out the relationships to your analysis. Point out the averages (or the mean, median, or mode), the ranges, the exceptions, and the trends. Describe the significance of what was presented.

Three special cautions are in order here about tables and graphics:

1. Be sure to introduce the display before it appears on the page. And, subordinate this introduction to place the emphasis on a significant fact rather than on the display itself.

   NOT: Table 3 shows that, of those people surveyed, seven out of ten would participate in the program.
   BUT: Seven out of ten of those people surveyed said they would participate in the program, as is shown in Table 3.

2. Be sure you have *interpreted* the table or graphic. Merely to describe or reiterate what can be read in the display would be to insult your reader's intelligence. Point out the significance of what is in the display as it contributes to your analysis.
   For example:
   The total expenditure for health care in the United States in that year was $45.5 billion, as is shown in Figure 1. This amount represents about 6 percent of the total gross national product. The total health care expenditures have been estimated to increase to $100 billion by the late 1970s. The total expenditure was divided between Federal and other public and private sources with the private sector of the economy the major source of the expenditure. Almost 92 percent of the total expenditures were for health services and supplies, while the remaining 8 percent was spent for research, development, and facilities construction. Of this 8 percent, which

amounted to $3.6 billion, $1.8 billion were used for research and development.

3. Be sure the display can stand alone; that is, if the display were removed from the report, neither would be dependent on the other. Untitled and unnumbered displays, such as a simple tabulation or listing, are exceptions to this guide. These displays are called "dependent tables" or "dependent graphics."

When you have completed the analysis and its presentation, evaluate the quality of what you have done by using these criteria:

Have you:

1. Rechecked your arithmetic for accuracy?
2. Used terms correctly and unambiguously?
3. Excluded trivia in your analysis?
4. Made sure units of different kinds are converted to a common base; e.g., metric tons, 1990 dollars?
5. Not mistaken correlation for causation?
6. Been as diligent about including negative data as you have for including positive date?
7. Searched for meaning using both quantitative and qualitative analysis?
8. Been cautious in ascribing accuracy to data?
9. Been alert to your bias and to that of your primary and secondary data sources?
10. Handled tense carefully so your reader can follow your point of view?

When you have completed the analysis and its evaluation, you are ready to write the chapter summary.

Summarizing the Chapter

The length of the chapter determines the amount of summarizing needed. A one-page summary for a seven- to ten-page chapter would, perhaps, appear too detailed and repetitious to your reader. And whether you use a caption to label the section as "Summary" or use introductory words to signal a summary to your reader is immaterial.

Arriving at a Subanswer

The purpose of this summary section is to resolve the contribution of your analysis toward answering a subproblem or accepting or rejecting your hypothesis. Thus, help your reader by pointing out this chapter's contribution to answering your problem. In essence, then, the section contains a *sub*conclusion. These chapter subconclusions, in turn, are combined and evaluated in the terminal chapter for an overall answer to your research problem. The following examples reflect to a degree the range in lengths of chapter summaries and the means for introducing them.

> On the basis of the foregoing analysis in this chapter, the hypothesis that fewer than half of the associations surveyed would not use computers is refuted. The data show 77 percent were computer users.
>
> Also, apparently the use or non-use of a computer is directly related to an association's size. The computer users' average size was $78 million in assets compared with $11 million average for the non-users.
>
> Since savings and loan associations apparently are using computers more than as originally thought, it is not significant to examine the types of applications they use. These data are presented next in Chapter 4.
>
> —Ralph McDonald, Arizona State University

Or:

> In summary, then, Phoenix was found to hold a relative advantage in four major areas in attracting manufacturers. The supply of labor suitable for manufacturing employment was ample. In-migration, the development of educational facilities, and native population growth have contributed to the development of an adaptable labor force. Phoenix held a market accessibility advantage over most metropolitan areas. The size of the Southwest market and the expansion of transporta-

tion facilities contributed to the Phoenix attractiveness. The noninventory tax, low unemployment tax rate, and sales and use tax exemptions reduced manufacturing costs. Climate was the single nonproductive factor considered advantageous to Phoenix.

Increasing land costs, the lack of direct international transportation, and a shortage of water were the major disadvantages of locating a manufacturing plant in Phoenix.

These results indicate that Phoenix economic planners and developers should stress the labor, tax, transportation, market accessibility, and climate factors in attempts to lure manufacturers to Phoenix. The effects of high land costs and water shortages should be minimized. With these factors now established, the manufacturing executives' opinions of the advantages and disadvantages of locating a manufacturing plant in Phoenix are evaluated in Chapter 5, next.

—Kenneth Megel, Arizona State University

Or:

Summary

The LP-gas industry is large and well established and has extensive storage and distribution facilities. It is well able to respond to an increasing market for vehicular fuel. LP-gas is abundantly available in steadily increasing quantities from domestic and import sources and by diversion from the petrochemical market.

Distributors in the Phoenix area sell fuel almost exclusively by refilling tanks periodically on customers' premises. The distributors are poorly located to compete with gasoline service stations.

The LP-gas installation of $400 to $700 per vehicle is normally offset by the lower price of LP-gas compared to gasoline. The price of LP-gas to an individual at the distributorship is currently equivalent to a gasoline price of 52.3 cents per gallon and is therefore more expensive than premium gasoline. [True when written, in 1973.]

Conversion of automobiles to LP-gas is not justified unless its price becomes competitive with gasoline or a gasoline shortage occurs. The events that could result in a shortage of gasoline are the principal topics of Chapter 4.

—Kenneth D. Probert, Arizona State University

Make sure your summary does not merely retrace what you have covered in the chapter. Instead, concentrate on reviewing the generalizations stemming from your analysis. What you say here in the form of subanswers provides the basis for arriving at the overall answer to your research in the terminal chapter. Just as you need to provide a signal to your reader that you have ended the analysis and are now presenting the chapter summary, so should you provide a transition for leaving one chapter and entering the next.

Providing a Chapter Transition

Chapter transitions skillfully constructed can lead the reader unobtrusively from chapter to chapter. Through a lack of skill, however, transitions can become awkward, obvious, and repetitive. An admonition here is that if the transitions cannot be handled skillfully, then one should leave them out rather than have them detract from the written presentation.

Both forward and backward looking transitions between two content chapters are shown in the following example.

CHAPTER 3

. . . .

Elements of
subconclusion

In summary, the program manager position has several characteristics that distinguish it from other management positions. Basically, the program manager must direct activities that require extensive participation by organizations and agencies outside his immediate control.

. . . .

In today's large multi-program organizations where the management of a single program may cut across functional lines of authority, these management principles are simply not adequate. A strong need exists to provide a discrete differentiation between the functional-manager and program-manager spheres of influence. Program authority, as a conceptual framework, makes such a differentiation possible.

Forward-looking transition

In chapter 4, next, authority relationships in an actual matrix organization are analyzed to ascertain the practical significance of the program authority concepts presented in this chapter.

CHAPTER 4

Chapter Title

Backward-looking transition

Actual program authority relationships in a matrix organization, discussed conceptually in the preceding chapter, are examined and evaluated in this chapter. Primary data for this examination were obtained by means of a questionnaire survey conducted at a firm utilizing a matrix organization.

Objectives as a forward-looking transition

The chapter objectives are to (1) determine the nature of, (2) quantitatively measure, and (3) deduce the probable causes for authority conflicts in a matrix organization. Design parameters of the questionnaire are presented, and the method used in conducting the survey is described. Last, the survey results are tabulated and analyzed.

—Eugene A. Krueger, Arizona State University

The completion of the analysis phase, along with its written presentation, leads to the terminal phase of the research, as described next in Chapter 9.

9

Writing the Terminal Chapter

The terminal chapter of a research project is the culmination of the analysis presented in the content chapters. Here the researcher accumulates the subanswers and resolves them into an overall answer to the research problem that was posed in the "Introduction." Also, this terminal chapter provides the researcher an opportunity for a final conference with the reader to assure all commitments promised in the beginning have been met.

The structure of the terminal chapter often poses a dilemma for the researcher regarding what should be included and where to place that which is included. For example, should a summary of the previous chapters be included? If a summary is included, what is the relationship to the conclusions? Do they overlap and become redundant? Should implications of the research be discussed? Are recommendations for further research appropriate for nonacademic research? These are the kinds of questions that appear to be most bothersome to the researcher.

An approach for writing the terminal chapter is described in the following sections:

1. Structuring the summary section
2. Developing and presenting the conclusions
3. Presenting the research implications and recommendations

Structuring the Summary Section

The length of the research project probably is the main consideration in deciding whether to include a summary in the terminal chapter. And here we must be sure the character of a summary is set out. A *summary* is a condensation of the major points—no more, no less; it is only a review. A *conclusion*, however, resolves the major points to an answer to the research problem.

Your concern should be to provide reader convenience and ease in understanding, but not at the expense of monotonous repetition. If you have done a good job of showing the contribution of the content chapters in their summaries, then an overall summary may be repetitious in the terminal chapter.

If you decide an overall summary is needed, then use a direct approach for structuring the chapter. Following are guides for writing the summary:

1. Use a deductive approach by presenting in the first sentence your overall answer to your research problem.
2. Use a whipback transition to pick up your research problem and method, as shown in Figure 9.1. This method quickly and effectively orients your reader to the problem, method, and answer, and it avoids the

mystery-novel approach that is so irritating to the reader of a research report.

3. Summarize the remaining chapters in sequence; maintain the chapter proportion in the summary.
4. Follow with the specific conclusions; itemize them for emphasis and clarity.

The following is an example of the approach shown in Figure 9.1.

Summary and Conclusions

The shortage of transportation fuels resulting from the extensive energy crisis may have a significant effect on the aerospace industry for many years to come. The effects are differ-

FIGURE 9.1

Structure of a Summary in the Terminal Chapter

CHAPTER NUMBER

Chapter Title

Overall answer to problem

Summary

Summary of first chapter
Summary of second chapter
Summary of third chapter
(and so on)

Conclusions

Itemize the specific conclusions

ent for each of the major segments of the aerospace industry, but overall the industry promises to meet the challenge of the energy crisis and prosper from it in the long run. The short-term prospect is for mildly constrained growth until long-term research and development efforts become fruitful.

Summary

The foregoing conclusions stem from a study of the problem: What potential effects will limited supplies of transportation fuels due to the energy crisis have on the aerospace industry? Secondary data from the Hayden Library and Sperry Flight Systems, consisting of government documents, aerospace trade association publications, and periodicals were collected and analyzed: (1) to determine the nature and extent of the energy crisis; (2) to determine the energy crisis effects on the commercial aircraft market; (3) to evaluate the general aviation situation; and (4) to determine the reactions by the government-funded military, space, and R & D sectors of the aerospace industry.

    The potential for a crisis, as examined in Chapter 2, existed in 1969 when the United States petroleum production. . . .
       —Michael A. Mason, Arizona State University

If you have structured your research report with only one content chapter, then the research answer probably is apparent at the end of that chapter. Thus, minimize the treatment of the content chapter summary and give the major emphasis in the terminal chapter. Even then, you are not likely to want a summary in the terminal chapter; rather, conclusions only will serve better.

Developing and Presenting the Conclusions

Your overall conclusion is the answer to your research problem as stated in the "Introduction." It is the answer you derive through analysis of the collected data. Whether you have one or several content chapters, the process of deriving the conclusion is the same. The process is reflected graphically in Figure 9.2.

FIGURE 9.2

Structuring the Conclusions in the Terminal Chapter

(Only one content chapter)   (Two or more content chapters)

II. Chapter Title   II. First Content Chapter
    A. First Section

Data and analysis
Subanswer A

Data and analysis for each section
Chapter subanswer

    B. Second section   III. Second Content Chapter

Data and analysis
Subanswer B

Data and analysis for each section
Chapter subanswer

    C. Third section   IV. Conclusion Chapter

Data and analysis
Subanswer C

Resolve chapter sub-answers II and III to overall answer to problem

III. Conclusion Chapter

Resolve subanswers A, B, and C to overall answer to the problem

Thus, through a reasoning process in your analysis you have derived a series of mini-answers. These mini or sub-answers furnish the basis for your conclusion in the manner of:

because 1	(subanswer 1)
because 2	(subanswer 2)
because 3	(subanswer 3)
therefore	conclusion

Based upon the foregoing description, here is a guide for presenting the conclusions:

A. If a summary is *included* in this chapter:
   1. Follow the summary material as described on page 135, with a heading labeled "Conclusions."
   2. If the subanswers from the content sections need resolving to the overall answer, do so here.
   3. Set out the specific conclusions in itemized format.
   4. Follow each listed conclusion with any interpretation, limitations, or conditions as needed.
B. If a summary is *omitted* from this chapter:
   1. Present the generalized, overall research answer in the first sentence as was done in item 1 in "Structuring the Summary."
   2. Provide a transition back to your problem statement and method; recap these elements quickly.
   3. Follow the practices set out in items 2, 3, and 4 under A above.
C. For the conclusions section in general:
   1. Be sure the summary and conclusions are differentiated, preferably through using headings. At the least, you can separate them by paragraphing.
   2. The conclusions should be clearly set out and should follow from the analysis presented.
   3. The questions or objectives given in the "Introduction" must be answered or met.
   4. No *new* data or evidence may be presented; thus, footnotes are not likely to appear in this section.

Following is an example of a conclusions section that did not include a summary.

Conclusions and Recommendations

Pipelines carrying solids can and should have a role in a transportation system and an overall economic scheme. This role, however, will be limited by technical and economic constraints. This conclusion is based upon an analysis of three subproblems designed to determine: (1) the advantages and disadvantages of solids lines; (2) what has been and is being done in the field of solids transport via pipelines; (3) the advances and conditions necessary to make the pipeline transport of solids more feasible.

The research on solids pipelines was confined to the secondary materials found in the Hayden and Architecture Libraries at Arizona State University and to three national companies knowledgeable in the area.

Conclusions

Solids pipelines' definite, although currently limited, role in an economic scheme can be deduced from the following evidence as sub-conclusions developed in this study:

1. Pipelines, in general, and particularly solids pipelines, possess a number of advantages that assist them in providing relatively low delivered costs. These distinct advantages are: (a) stability and reliability; (b) relative insulation from inflationary trends; and (c) low labor requirements.
2. The feasibility of solids is influenced by two sets of mitigating factors. A dearth of technical knowledge and economic constraints limit their viability.
3. Solids pipelines have been successfully utilized for over one hundred years. They have proven their practicability in a number of world locations and have carried a vast array of materials—many of which would have otherwise been unusable.
4. To expand the currently limited role of solids pipelines, research must be undertaken into the technical aspects of solids transmission, especially capsules. Also, the economic conditions affecting solids lines must be analyzed and understood.

Thus, through evaluation of the areas presented in the preceding conclusion, frameworks of thought concerning the role of solids pipelines in an economic scheme can be formulated. Overall, solids pipelines do have a place in a transportation system and a total economic scheme; the extent of this role is limited by technical and economic factors.

—Michael W. Carnahan, Arizona State University

With the conclusions established, your thoughts now turn to the research implications, or recommendations, or both.

Presenting the Research Implications and Recommendations

No clear-cut guide can be given for structuring the implications and recommendations for your research. What you do will depend upon what those who will review or receive your research report expect from you. For example, if your research has been done to meet degree requirements, you may be considered presumptuous to offer recommendations for action. This belief stems from the idea that research of universal value should not recommend; rather, those in the field (the practitioners) will recommend action based upon your conclusions. In this instance, then, you would be in good standing to offer *implications* attending your conclusions. Implications point out for your readers the "so what" of your results. Thus, one may generalize that for academic-type research (universal benefits) you would offer implications. For restricted-use research (company, institutions, or organizations), you would develop recommendations for action, unless, of course, you discern recommendations are unwelcome. One thing certain here is that any recommendations for action must derive from the conclusions presented if they are to be creditable.

In either instance, universal or restricted use, you may be expected to offer recommendations for further research. Since you may now be considered to be the "mini authority" in this specific area of research, you should be the one to offer suggestions for new avenues of investigation or changes in approach. Following are examples of implications and recommendations.

Implications

The implications stemming from the analysis of the data in this study might indicate that the State Compensation Fund Loss Prevention Department does not maintain the proper information or of a type to define the accident process adequately. Yet, these data are all that can be generated with the current system of reporting by the policyholders of the State Compensation Fund.

If the Loss Prevention Department is to develop accident-reducing programs that will affect the cost of the accidents, the policyholders will have to provide more data for analysis. Until such time, as inexact as the information may be, valid results may still be generated by utilizing the safety programs already developed to reduce accident frequency on dairy farms. Also, the excess frequencies or variability on chi square analysis might indicate poor worker environment or poor management-worker interaction.

—Robert J. Ekiss, Arizona State University

From a study profiling a zoo membership to establish a marketing strategy come these recommendations for action.

Recommendations for Action

To best meet the needs and desires of existing members and incorporate potential markets into the marketing direction, the following strategies are recommended.

1. Continue a family-oriented marketing program but gear some promotions and benefits to the large, single market.
2. Plan educational programs, entertainment, and special promotions to include all age levels of children.
3. Stress the benefits and low cost of a membership to middle-income families to prove it is inside their price range.
4. Gear promotions and events to accommodate better the high income, well-educated existing members through the use of more educational material.
5. Encourage repeat attendance and stimulate long-standing members who are nonattenders by frequently changing exhibits and programs.
6. Continue with the present policy of issuing six guest passes with each membership.
7. Stress the conservation and preservation philosophy of the zoo in advertising and promotional campaigns.
8. Consider including more sightseeing trips, lectures and films, and children's nature classes into existing membership benefits.
9. Provide accessible information and displays on the zoo grounds to promote membership.

10. Capitalize on the high response to publicity by making maximum use of zoo stories and events.
—Mary Nicholson, Arizona State University

A study on the current uses of comparative advertising offered these recommendations for further research.

Recommendations for Further Research

To determine more precisely the effectiveness of comparative advertising, further research must be conducted. Future experiments should be closely controlled and should test the comparative approach using a wide variety of copy forms and technical strategies. Printed ads and television commercials have received most of the research attention thus far—radio has been virtually ignored. This oversight is somewhat disturbing, considering the great importance of radio as an advertising medium. Obviously, that which makes a television commercial effective may not necessarily do the same for a radio spot.

In addition to expanded laboratory research, extensive consumer surveys should be conducted. Most opinion polls taken to date have questioned advertising executives and business leaders, but few surveys have sought the opinions of those most directly influenced by a comparative message. Again, this void is quite surprising. Nearly all advertising efforts are directed toward the ultimate consumer, but unless consumer reactions to comparative advertising are clearly understood, the use of such an approach may prove to be a somewhat hazardous venture.
—Allan C. Mayer, Jr., Arizona State University

Overall, structuring this chapter requires as much creativity as does the "Introduction." It is not to be a mere rehash of what has gone before, with the idea of letting the readers make of it what they will. The terminal chapter or section should be the result of reflective thinking about the project and leave no doubt about the specific contribution of the research.

10
Achieving a Scholarly Writing Style

The purpose of this chapter is to furnish a reference for good word choice and use and the mechanics for presenting them in scholarly writing. As viewed here, the following factors are involved in scholarly writing:

1. Making writing clear;
2. Eliminating deadwood in writing;
3. Managing sentences and paragraphs.

Making Writing Clear

A mature writing style and clear writing doesn't just happen; it requires a deliberate effort involving precision, good taste, and good manners. A "good" style in writing may be defined as that which accomplishes the writer's purpose without calling attention to the words or constructions used.

The words people choose in writing are what readers use as a criterion in judging them. Words represent the personality, character, and education of the person using them.

Use the Right Word

One of the first requirements of words in scholarly writing is that they be in "good use," which use implies acceptance by the majority of authorities. To be accepted, the word choice must be exact, reputable, and modern. The following list contains the words that are frequently *misused* in report writing.

above, below
Don't use *above* as an adjective in constructions such as "the *above* statement." Too frequently the *above* and *below* references appear on the previous or following pages, which makes the references illogical. Better to say "the foregoing statement" or "the following list."

affect, effect
To *affect* means to produce an *effect*, to have influence upon; *effect* means the immediate result, that which is produced by a cause. "The new model *affected* total sale." "The *effect* on sales was caused by the new model."

although, while
Although means "in spite of the fact that" or "even though." *While* is generally accepted to mean "during the time that" or "at the same time." "*Although* (not *while*) both banks are growing significantly in assets, . . ." (but) "These forms can be filled out *while* (at the same time) the teller is completing a transaction. "Also, note that *while* should not be used for coordinate ideas that need *and* or *but*. "Form A serves only the function of evaluating the employees *but* (not *while*) form B often provides too much information."

amount, number, proportion
Amount refers to quantity, bulk, mass; *number* refers to countable units. *Proportion* is a ratio, the relation of one part

to another. The *amount* of water in the ocean; the *amount* of energy expended in a game. *Number* of gallons; the *number* of people; the *proportion* of men and women in the company's employ.

and/or
And/or is a legalism; avoid using it. Don't write "this change may cause a reduction in hours *and/or* pay." Instead, write "This change may cause a reduction in hours, or pay, or both."

anticipate, expect
Anticipate should not be used in place of *expect*. Synonyms for *anticipate* are *prevent* and *foresee*. Synonyms for *expect* are *hope* and *look*. "He *anticipated* the computer installation by completing a course in computer programming." "We *expect* that the time savings will release four employees for other work."

as to
As to is a substitute for a simple preposition, and it shouldn't be used to introduce words that could stand without it.
NOT: "They aren't sure *as to* the proposed change."
BUT: "They aren't sure *about* the proposed change."
NOT: "There was doubt as to whether to adopt the policy."
BUT: "There was doubt *whether* to adopt the policy."

author, writer
Stylistic preference today frowns on the use of "the author" or "the writer" to refer to the person conducting an investigation or experiment. Simply restructuring the sentence can eliminate such references.
NOT: "The author developed a questionnaire to . . ."
BUT: "A questionnaire was developed to . . ."

balance, remainder
Balance should not be used as a substitute for *remainder* in formal writing except in accounting terms. *Balance* has the meaning of equilibrium, whereas *remainder* means residue,

that left over. "The account now has a credit *balance*." "The *remainder* of the accounts was given to an attorney for collection."

believe, feel
To *believe* is to think, to judge, to have convictions. To *feel* is to touch, to examine, to be aware of an impression. "They *believe* (not *feel*) this year will be a good sales year."

better than, more than
Better than is colloquial when used in place of *more than.* "*More than* (not *better than*) fifty trials were made."

bimonthly
Bimonthly means every two months. It has also come to mean twice a month. For clarity, discard the word and write "every two months" or "twice a month." Leave no room for doubt about what is meant.

case
The word *case* has many legitimate uses, but so often it is used when it contributes no meaning to an expression. *Case* is a frequent source of jargon in writing.

Don't Write:	*Write:*
in all cases	always
in case	if
in cases where	when
in most cases	usually
in some cases	sometimes
in which case	then
this being the case	thus; so

conclusion, summary
These words are not synonymous. *Conclusion* is an answer derived by reasoning; it is a decision or opinion resulting from an investigation. A *summary* is a brief review of the main points in a presentation. Thus, in report writing, analysis and reasoning must be present to conclude; a summary,

though, is not dependent upon reasoning since it is a review only.

data
Data is the plural of *datum.* Precision in writing requires the use of a plural verb with *data* except when the meaning applies to a collection of data as a unit. "These data indicate. . . ." "The data in this research comes from three sources (as a unit)."

different from, different than
Different than is considered substandard usage. Use *different from.* "This machine is *different from* (not *different than*) the one used before." But, also notice: "This machine is *larger than* the one used before."

enormity, enormousness
These words are not interchangeable. *Enormousness* means huge; a great size in number or degree. *Enormity* means wicked, vicious, or immoderate. The use of *enormity* to mean vastness or great size is considered substandard usage.

etc.
Etc. means "and other things." It is also used for "and so forth." Proper usage would be at the end of an almost completed list or for immaterial words at the end of a quote. Do *not* use etc. to end a sentence beginning with "such as," "for example," or any similar expressions. Don't force your reader to fill in details you are unable or unwilling to do.

fewer, less
In general, use *fewer* for number and *less* for degree or amount. *Fewer* (not *less*) people, *fewer* books, *fewer* dollars. *Less* gasoline (but *fewer* gallons of gasoline), *less* time, *less* energy.

forego, forgo
To *forego* something is to precede it; to go before. To *forgo* something is to go without; to abstain. Thus, the salad *fore-*

goes the main course (precedes), and you may *forgo* the dessert (go without).

however
Prefer not to start a sentence with *however* when *nevertheless* is meant.
NOT: "*However,* these definitions are imprecise."
BUT: "These definitions, *however,* are imprecise."

imply, infer
Imply is to involve as a necessary condition. *Infer* is to derive by reasoning. A speaker or writer *implies*; the listener or reader *infers*. I *imply* by what I say, and I *infer* from what you say.

irregardless
Nonstandard English. Use **regardless.**

method, methodology, procedure
Method is orderly procedure or manner of doing something. *Methodology* is a branch of logic concerned with principles of procedure. *Procedure* is a manner or method of proceeding. A *method*, therefore, is an application of *methodology*. And, no difference in meaning is evident between *method* and *procedure*; so, the combined use of *"methods and procedures"* in a report is redundant. The term *methodology* as is often used in reports is a genteelism—pompous phrasing.

on the other hand
Used by itself, this term is trite. Not: *"On the other hand,* their price is better." Correct use is: *"On the one hand, . . . on the other hand, . . ."*

only
Misplacing the modifier *only* in a sentence can change meaning. Place *only* before the word it modifies. Notice the changes in meaning in the following:
Elko paints cars.
Only Elko paints cars. (no other company paints cars)
Elko *only* paints cars. (Elko doesn't repair or service cars)
Elko paints *only* cars. (Elko doesn't paint boats or machinery)

parameter, perimeter

A *parameter* is a variable, a characteristic, or a factor.
A *perimeter* is a boundary or a circumference. *Parameter* is frequently misused as meaning "boundary."

presently, at present

Presently means *soon; at present* means *now.* Don't write "Two employees are *presently* working in the mail room."

reason is because

Because means "for the reason that"; so one is actually saying "reason is for the reason that."

NOT: "The *reason* we are not participating is *because* of the cost factor."

BUT: "The *reason* we are not participating is the cost factor."

that, which

The relative pronouns *that* and *which* are not always interchangeable. *That* restricts, limits, or defines the word or phrase preceding it. *That* pertains to persons, animals, or things. *Which* expands the meaning of the preceding word or phrase. *Which* pertains *only* to animals or things. "The program *that* John developed has been in use for five years." The pronoun *that* restricts the meaning of the word *program* to the one that John developed. The idea introduced by *that* could *not* be removed without losing the meaning of the sentence. Notice that commas are *not* used to set off the *that* idea. "The incentive program, *which* was developed five years ago, has increased production 32 percent." Here the pronoun *which* merely expands the meaning by adding a new thought. The idea introduced by *which* could be deleted without losing the meaning of the sentence. Also, notice that commas are used to enclose the *which* idea.

true fact

A *fact* is generally defined as "something that actually happened or is true." The term *true fact*, then, is a redundancy because if something *isn't* true, it isn't a fact.

Eliminating Deadwood in Writing

Most of us tend to give our readers more than they need. We write with a dull and pompous style. Sometimes we know something is wrong but don't know what it is. Elements involved, generally, here are: redundancies, long connectives, expletive beginnings, cliches, Latin and legal terms, and stylish words.

Recognize Redundancies

A redundancy is a word or phrase that repeats an idea already expressed—a misused form of emphasis. The following redundancies are found frequently in report writing.

Don't Write:	Write:
accordingly and consequently	(one; not both)
advance planning	planning
assemble together	assemble
basic fundamentals	fundamentals
but nevertheless	(one; not both)
close scrutiny	scrutiny
conclude at the end	conclude
consensus of opinion	(one; not both)
controversial issue	issue
each and every	(one; not both)
evident and apparent	(one; not both)
exactly identical	identical
first and foremost	(one; not both)
important essentials	essentials
initial beginning	beginning
lag behind	lag
legal and lawful	(one; not both)
necessary requirement	requirement
new innovation	innovation
other alternative	alternative
past experience	experience
refer back	refer

rules and regulations	(one; not both)
still continues	continues
sum total	(one; not both)
true facts	facts
whether or not	whether

Eliminate Long Connectives

Padded writing serves only to irritate a reader. Note how the phrases on the left are slow and plodding. The substitutes on the right carry your reader along swiftly to your ideas with no loss in meaning.

Wordy:	*Concise:*
almost never	seldom
along the lines of	like
are in agreement	agree
are of the opinion that	believe
arrived at the conclusion that	concluded
as related to	for; about
at all times	always
at the present time	now
at this point in time	now
by means of	by
be in a position to	can
despite the fact that	though
during the course of	during
during the time that	while
each particular time	each time
few and far between	seldom
for the period of	for
for the reason that	since; because
in a position to	able
in light of the fact that	although
in the majority of instances	usually
in other words	thus; so
in view of the fact that	since
it would appear	apparently

most of the time	usually
never before in the past	never
on or before	by
prior to	before
sometime in the near future	soon
subsequent to	after
to summarize the above	in summary
until such time as	until
with the exception of	except
with regard to	about

Avoid Expletive Beginnings

An expletive in writing is a word or phrase not needed for meaning but just used to fill out a sentence. Expletive beginnings are slow and wordy; they put the subject far along in the sentence and delay meaning for your reader. Some expletive sentence starts are: *it is, it was, there is, there are,* and *there were.* Recast such sentences for clarity and conciseness.

NOT: *"It is* the purpose of this report . . ."
BUT: "The purpose of this report is . . ."
NOT: *"There are* five steps that should be taken . . ."
BUT: "Five steps should be taken . . ."
NOT: *"It is* the opinion of the surveyors that . . ."
BUT: "The surveyors believe . . ."

Eliminate Cliches

Cliches are terms that have become wearisome and monotonous through their overuse or because using them leads to other communication problems. They help to destroy clarity; so, avoid using them by substituting a word for the cliche or by leaving them out.

a well known fact	goes without saying
along these lines	in the business world of
any way, shape, or form	today
ballpark figure	in the final analysis
bone of contention	in the foreseeable future

bottom line
by the same token
conspicuous by its absence
educated guess
exception that proves the rule
few and far between
final analysis
foregone conclusion

interesting to note
needless to say
last but not least
needs no introduction
simple reason that
too numerous to mention
viable alternative

Discard Latin and Legal Terms

Latin and legal terms are of questionable use in scholarly writing because they usually are unfamiliar, laborious, and pompous to a reader. They are likely to *sound* impressive but carry no meaning. Help a reader by translating them.

Instead of Writing:	*Why Not Write:*
a priori	from cause to effect
ad hoc	temporary
and/or	(forget it)
be cognizant of	be aware of, know, notice
ceteris paribus	other things being equal
execute	complete
exercise	use
infra	below, following
in lieu of	instead of
modus operandi	procedure
nota bene	notice well
per annum	yearly
per diem	daily
pursuant to	following
said	this
subject	this
supra	above, earlier
vis-a-vis	face-to-face
viz	namely

And, avoid using a pseudo legal style in writing:
NOT: "two (2) months' supply
BUT: "two months' supply"

NOT: "eight (8) percent less"
BUT: "eight percent less"
NOT: "In the case of the Scottsdale area . . ."
BUT: "For the Scottsdale area . . ."

Use Working Words

Stylish words (genteelisms) cause writing to be dull, uninteresting, and difficult to read and understand. Some people believe readers like elegant writing and that these readers will think one is uneducated and undignified if the writing doesn't sound impressive. Stylish words aren't necessarily bad, but they're bad when a writer uses them to the exclusion of simple ones. Be assured your IQ is not measured by the length of your words.

The following list provides examples of choosing a simple substitute for a multi-syllable word. Note that the stylish words are three or more syllables, and the working words are one or two syllables.

Stylish words:	Working words:
accordingly	so
approximately	about
characteristic	trait
compensation	pay
concerning	about
consumate	close
demonstrate	show
discontinue	stop
enumerate	list
expenditure	payment
foundation	base
fundamental	basic
inadvisable	risky
indication	sign
indispensable	vital
industrious	busy
materialize	appear
modification	change
possibility	chance

recapitulate	review
remuneration	pay
transformation	change
unadulterated	pure
verification	proof

Managing Sentences and Paragraphs

Writing good sentences requires patience, technique, and feeling; it's a job for which we need diligence, concentration, and practice. Good sentences and paragraphs don't result from just stringing words together as they tumble from our minds; they must be controlled and fashioned into acceptable form and style. The following principles are the ones violated frequently in report writing: pronoun reference, parallelism, transitions, emphasis, sexism, and punctuation.

Have a Clear Pronoun Reference

Every pronoun must stand for a word that has already been expressed; and what it stands for must be evident immediately. A vague pronoun whose meaning appears later in the sentence irritates a reader.

NOT: Sample letters should be selected periodically, and a critique of each letter should be made. *This* will require the services of a correspondence specialist.

BUT: Sample letters should be selected periodically, and a critique of each letter should be made. *This critique* will require the services of a correspondence specialist.

NOT: Approximately eight full-time employees are needed on the dietary staff. *This* is indicated since Standard (B) is not met.

BUT: Approximately eight full-time employees are needed on the dietary staff. *This need* is indicated since Standard (B) is not met.

NOT: The *company* is apathetic about *their* customers.

BUT: The *company* is apathetic about *its* customers.

Express Parallel Ideas in Parallel Form

Logic requires parallel grammatical construction for parallel ideas. Otherwise, the structure causes momentary confusion and annoyance.

NOT: The property is still being used for farming and a citrus grove.
BUT: The property is still being used for farming and growing citrus.
NOT: Writing is sometimes more effective than to give instructions orally.
BUT: Writing is sometimes more effective than giving instructions orally.
NOT: The duties of the administrator are: (1) presiding at all meetings, (2) to call special meetings, and (3) responsibility for appointing committees.
BUT: The duties of the administrator are to: (1) preside at all meetings, (2) call special meetings, and (3) appoint committees.

Provide Transitions

Use roadsigns effectively for transitions. Don't force the reader to make the shifts alone.

To add:	further, moreover, besides, also, in addition
To contrast:	but, however, yet, on the contrary
To compare:	similarly, in the same way
To show time:	before this, then, a month later, now, later on
To show consequence:	as a result, therefore, accordingly, thus, for this reason
To close:	in summary, in brief, in short

Use Emphasis Effectively

Some ways of emphasizing in report writing are:

- by underscoring words: "You *think* you are right."
- by placement: put key ideas in lead-off position or end position. Play down ideas by putting them in unemphatic middle spots.
- by *saying* something is important.
- by controlling the amount of space used. The more space devoted to an idea, the more emphasis achieved.
- by sentence length and pattern. In general, stylists recommend a twenty-word sentence average for easy reading. This figure suggests that some sentences may be only a few words and others may be forty or fifty words. To tell writers to keep *all* sentences short would result in monotony and primer-style writing. Sentence length and variety in sentence pattern are closely related. Provide variety by using simple, complex, compound, and compound-complex sentence patterns. And, don't end up with a sausage-link string of subject-verb-object sentence structures; use some introductory-phrase and -clause constructions, too.

Avoid Sexist Constructions

Careful writers avoid sex-role stereotyping in their writing; they afford men and women equal treatment. Following are suggestions for reflecting a sexually unbiased attitude in writing.

1. Drop the male pronoun "he" and "his" from the construction.
   NOT: The depositor retains his copy of the deposit slip.
   BUT: The depositor retains a copy of the deposit slip.

2. Use a plural construction.
   NOT: An executive is a busy person. He appreciates brevity in what he must read.
   BUT: Executives are busy people. They appreciate brevity in what they must read.

3. Use a genderless "person" or "one" construction.
   NOT: The wise report writer will use long words with

caution. He will make certain the long words he uses are well known to his reader.

BUT: The wise report writer will use long words with caution. That is, one must make certain the long words one uses are well known to the reader.

4. Avoid sex-role descriptors such as *girl, fairer sex, chairwoman, authoress,* and *stewardess.*
   NOT: Ask one of the girls to type it.
   BUT: Ask one of the secretaries to type it.

NOT	BUT
salesman	sales representative
early man	primitive people
businessman	business executive

And finally,

NOT: The good writer must become a student of words. He must learn the precise meaning of words.

BUT: The good writer must become a student of words. The precise meanings of words must be learned. (guide 1)

OR: Good writers must become students of words. They must learn the precise meanings of words. (guide 2)

OR: The good writer must become a student of words, one who learns the precise meanings of words. (guide 3)

Punctuate Correctly

Punctuation provides the signposts to meaning in a sentence. Any punctuation (or the lack of it) that causes a reader to back up and reread to get meaning has caused a problem. In some sentences, only by correct punctuation can the meaning be obtained at all. Reviewed here are some of the troublesome areas in punctuation.

1. Apostrophe
   a. Possessive pronouns do not take an apostrophe (its, theirs, yours, ours).

A Guide to Business Research

b. Even though ownership is not involved, the apostrophe is used for a week's time, a day's labor, two hours' travel.
c. Show individual or alternative possession with an apostrophe on each element of the series (students' or teachers' suggestions).
d. Show joint possession by placing an apostrophe on the last element of the series (accountants and lawyers' qualifications).

2. Colon
a. Use a colon to introduce any matter that forms a complete sentence, question, or quotation. (The following question came up for discussion: What policy should be adopted?)
b. Use a colon in proportions or ratios. (The concrete was mixed 5:3:1. The ratio was 1:2 :: 3:6.)

3. Comma
Of all the punctuation marks, the comma causes the most trouble. Mainly, the comma serves to show (1) parallel construction and (2) parenthetical elements.
Parallelism
a. Use a comma before the conjunction (*and, or, nor, but*) in a compound sentence with two independent clauses. (This stock is now $23, and it is not expected to go any lower.)
b. Don't use a comma between two verbs having the same subject.
NOT: "They obtained financing, and built the shopping center."
BUT: "They obtained financing and built the shopping center."
c. Use a comma after each item within a series of three or more words, phrases, letters, or figures used with *and, or, nor,* or *but* (by the week, by the month, or by the season or red, white, and blue).
d. Use a comma after each of a series of coordinate qualifying words (colorful, durable tile; but, colorful floor tile). If you can insert *and* between the elements or invert the order, you need a comma.

Parenthetical

e. Use a comma to set off a parenthetical element introduced by the conjunctions *because, as, if, although,
   when, after, as soon as,* and *such as.* (After I have read
   your report, I'll make a decision. When you have
   made your decision, let me know.)

f. Use a comma to set off parenthetic words, phrases, or
   clauses. (Their high morale might, he suggested,
   have caused them to win. But: The man who fell
   broke his back.)

g. Use commas to set off nonrestrictive phrases or
   clauses. (Grammar, which is a dull subject, is important.) If the statement would mean the same if
   the phrase or clause was left out, commas are
   needed.

h. Use commas to set off words or phrases in apposition
   or contrast. (Mr. Jones, the sales manager, made the
   request.)

i. Use commas to set off a noun used in a direct address.
   (Therefore, Mr. Smith, you'll want to take action
   now.)

Miscellaneous Uses

j. Use a comma to set off introductory elements in a
   sentence. Without the comma, the introductory portion would seem to run momentarily into the remainder of the sentence. (NOT: At the instant of starting the motor draws more than 200 amperes. BUT: At
   the instant of starting, the motor draws more than
   200 amperes.)

k. Use a comma to separate two words or figures that
   might otherwise be misunderstood. (In 1989, 240 employees were dismissed. OR: To Charles, John was
   ambitious.)

l. Don't use a comma between month and year in dates
   (June 1989; March, April, and May 1989).

4. Dash

   a. Use two hyphens to make a dash. Have no space be-
      fore or after the dash. (See examples in b, c, and d of
      this group.)

    b. Use a dash to mark a sudden break or abrupt change in thought. (If you are already using this system-- fine.)

    c. Use a dash as strong parentheses. (Some fuels currently are dominant--gas, oil, and coal--but solar energy use is near.)

    d. Use a dash before a final clause that summarizes a series of ideas. (Ability, maturity, and perseverance-- these are the qualities sought.)

    e. Don't use a dash as a substitute for a period, a semicolon, or a comma.

5. Ellipsis

    a. Use three spaced periods to indicate an ellipsis and four spaced periods when a sentence is brought to a close. Space before, between, and after the periods. (He ran . . . and won first place. OR: He ran . . . and won. . . .)

    b. Use a full line of spaced periods to show omission of one or more lines.

. . . .

6. Hyphen

    a. Use a hyphen to join two or more words into a single unit of modifiers preceding a noun (first-class plan; two-day affair; high-impact plastic; one-way street). Don't use a hyphen when the compound *follows* a noun. (The plan is first class. The plastic is high impact.)

    b. Omit the hyphen from compound adjectives when:

        1) the adjective is made from a commonly used two-word noun (an Indiana University student; an office machines salesperson).

        2) the first word of the compound is an adverb ending in -ly (a poorly constructed auto; a partly filled container).

        3) the compound is the name of a chemical (a copper sulphate solution).

7. Italics

    a. Show italics in typewriting by <u>underlining</u>.

    b. Underline the title of a periodical, a book, a booklet published under its own cover, a musical composition, the proper name of a ship, train, or airplane, or a foreign word (Business Week; Elements of Style; Concorde; et cetera).

8. Quotation Marks
   a. Place quotation marks outside the comma and period.
   b. Use quotation marks to enclose any matter following the words *entitled, the term, marked, endorsed,* or *signed.* (The check was endorsed "John Doe.")
   c. Use quotation marks at the *beginning* of each paragraph of a quotation, but at the *end* of the last paragraph only.
   d. Use quotation marks to enclose misnomers, slang expressions, or ordinary words used in an arbitrary way. (He spoke against the "lame duck" amendment.)
   e. Use quotation marks to enclose titles of essays, stories, poems, newspaper and magazine articles, and chapters of books.

9. Semicolon
   a. Use a semicolon to separate clauses containing commas. (When the space program was initiated, reentry was the principal difficulty; but this problem was solved some time ago.)
   b. Use a semicolon before and a comma after weak connectives when they connect two complete and related ideas. Such weak connectives are: *accordingly, also, hence, however, moreover, nevertheless, so, still, then, therefore, thus, yet.* (Unfamiliar words destroy clarity; therefore, prefer the familiar word to the far-fetched word.)
   c. Use a semicolon in place of a coordinating conjunction. (Accounting is one of the fastest growing professions today; the possibility of getting a job in accounting is very good.)

Appendix A: Collecting Data from Documentary Sources

The following reference books will tell you where to find information about business, such as indexes and bibliographies.

Basic Reference Sources by Louis Shores
Books in Print
Cumulative Book Index. 1898—
Encyclopedia of Business Information Sources. 1970
Guide to Reference Books by Constance Winchell
How to Use the Business Library by H. W. Johnson
Investment Information by James B. Way
Sources of Business Information by Edwin T. Coman

Bibliographies and Indexes

Accountant's Index
Agricultural Index

*Bibliography of Publications of University Bureaus of Business
     and Economic Research (AUBER)*
*Bibliographic Index: A Cumulative Bibliography of
     Bibliographies*
Business Education Index
Business Periodicals Index
Current Contents
Economic Abstracts
Education Index
Engineering Index
Funk & Scott International Index
Geography of Marketing: Resource Bibliography
Index to Economic Journals
Index to Legal Periodicals
International Bibliography of Economics
International Index to Periodical Literature
New York Times Index
Psychological Abstracts
Public Affairs Information Service, Bulletin
Readers' Guide to Periodical Literature
Social Sciences and Humanities Index
Subject Index to Periodicals
*Systems and Procedures Including Office Management;
     Information Sources*
Wall Street Journal Index

Research Completed Sources

A thorough search for research completed requires examination of
the following publications. These reviews may be supplemented by
commercial specialized searches such as *Datrix, Dialog,* and *SDC/
INFORM,* as are described later.

Academy of Management Journal (September issue)
Accounting Review (January issue)
American Economic Review (September issue)
American Economist (Spring issue)
Appraisal Journal (Spring issue)
*AUBER (Index of Publications of University Bureaus of Business
     and Economic Research)*
Business Education Index
Business Horizons (each issue)
Dissertation Abstracts

Doctoral Dissertations Accepted by American Universities
Guide to Lists of Masters Theses
International Business Research: Past, Present, and Future
Journal of Business (January issue)
Journal of Finance (March issue)
Journal of Marketing
Journal of Marketing Research
Masters Abstracts
Masters Theses in Education

Fact Books

Directory of Post Offices
Electronic News Financial Fact Book and Directory
Million Dollar Directory (Dun & Bradstreet)
Official Congressional Directory
Statistical Abstract of the U.S.
Stock Factographs
Thomas' Register of American Manufacturers
Yearbook of Agriculture

Dictionaries and Encyclopedias

Accountant's Encyclopedia
Current Abbreviations
Dictionary of Accountants
Dictionary of Foreign Trade
Dictionary of Modern Economics
Dictionary of Occupational Titles
Dictionary of Scientific and Technical Words
Encyclopedia of Advertising
Encyclopedia of Banking and Finance
Encyclopedia of Social Sciences (Revised Edition)
Encyclopedia of Tax Procedures
Exporters Encyclopedia
Glossary of Terms in Computers and Data Processing
Insurance Words and Their Meaning
Thomson's Dictionary of Banking

Yearbooks

American Yearbook
Credit Management Yearbook

Economic Almanac
Europa Yearbook
Management Almanac
Municipal Yearbook
Pan-American Yearbook
World Almanac

Suppose you have reviewed the card catalog and the appropriate indexes from the foregoing list using the key words in your research topic. And, suppose you have found only a few potential books and journal articles. A help at this point, then, is the U.S. Library of Congress, Subject Cataloging Division book *Subject Headings Used in the Dictionary Catalog of the Library of Congress.* This book lists subject headings with cross-references to other possible headings. Its use can open up a whole new range of sources to you. For example, suppose your topic area for research is *job satisfaction.* If you look up *job satisfaction* in this book, you will find these subdivisions.

Job Satisfaction
      xx Attitude (Psychology)
          Employee morale
          Labor and laboring classes
          Personnel management
          Satisfaction
          Work

Now you can review the indexes again using these new headings as possible leads to data sources. Next, go back to *Subject Headings* and look up each of the headings you noted under *Job satisfaction*, as just listed. Under each of these headings you will find additional potential headings to use in reviewing the indexes . . . all related to *job satisfaction.* For example, under the heading

      xx Attitude (Psychology) are listed these subheadings:
          Attitude change
          Conformity
          Dogmatism
          Empathy
          Frustration
          Job satisfaction
          Public opinion
          Scale analysis
          Stereotype

xx Emotions
Psychology
Public opinion
Set (psychology)
Social psychology
Testing

Thus, using the Library of Congress *Subject Headings Dictionary Catalog* furnished us with at least 170 potential headings related to *job satisfaction* to use in searching the indexes.

Special Documentary Searches

Government publications are an important source of data for business students. These federal government publications are not indexed in the card catalog; instead, review the documents in the following publications:

Business Conditions Digest
Census of Business
Census of Manufacturers
Census of Population
Census of Transportation
Checklist of International Business Publications
County Business Patterns
Economic Indicators
Federal Research Bulletin
Foreign Trade Reports
Government Research Announcements
Industry Reports
Marketing Information Guide U.S. (Department of Commerce)
Monthly Catalog (Comprehensive listing of government
    publications)
Monthly Labor Review
*Official Summary of Security Transactions and Holdings
    Reported to the SEC*
Overseas Business Reports
Quarterly Financial Report for Manufacturing Corporations
*Securities Traded on Exchanges Under the Securities
    Exchange Act*
Statistical Bulletin
U.S. Department of Commerce Publications
U.S. Industrial Outlook

Periodicals and Associations

This section contains listings of periodicals and associations categorized by general area of study. Associations often are valuable to help in furnishing guidance and data sources in research projects, especially when they may share in the research results.

Accounting Periodicals

Accounting Forum
Accounting Review
CPA Journal
Internal Auditor
Journal of Accountancy
Journal of Accounting Research
Management Accounting
Management Adviser
National Public Accountant

Accounting Associations

American Institute of Certified Public Accountants
National Association of Accountants
National Society of Public Accountants

Data Processing Periodicals

Automation Magazine
Business Automation
Computer Decisions
Computer Design
Computers and Automation and People
Computers and Information Systems
Computerworld
Data Management
Datamation
Data Processing Magazine
Epic
Infosystems
Journal of Systems Management

Data Processing Associations

Association for Computer Machinery
Association for Systems Management

Data Processing Management Association
National Microfilm Association

Economics Periodicals

American Economic Review
American Economist
American Journal of Agricultural Economics
Antitrust Law and Economic Review
Business and Economic Dimensions
Business Conditions Digest
Business Economics
Econometrica Economic Record
International Economic Review
Journal of Industrial Economics
Journal of Political Economy
Journal of Taxation
Labor Law Journal
Land and Water Law Review
Land Economics
Monthly Labor Review
National Tax Journal
OECD Observer
Quarterly Journal of Economics
Quarterly Review of Economics and Business
Review of Economics and Statistics
Review of Social Economy
Taxes

Economics Associations

American Economic Association
American Water Resources Association
National Association of Regulatory Utility Commissioners
Water Pollution Control Federation

Finance Periodicals

Bank Administration Magazine
Bankers Magazine
Bankers Monthly
Banking: Journal of the American Bankers Assoc.
Barron's Weekly

Burroughs Clearing House
Commercial and Financial Chronicle
Consumer Credit Leader
Credit and Financial Management
Dun's
Federal Reserve Bank of New York, Monthly Review
Federal Reserve Bulletin
Finance and Development
Financial Analysts Journal
Financial Executive
Financial Management
Financial World
Fundscope
Journal of Bank Research
Journal of Commercial Bank Lending
Journal of Finance
Journal of Money, Credit, and Banking
Magazine of Wall Street

Finance Associations

American Bankers Association
Financial Analysts Federation
Financial Executives Institute
International Bankers Association
National Association of Credit Management
National Association of Mutual Savings Banks
Securities Industry Association

General Business Periodicals

Air Conditioning, Heating & Refrigeration News
American Druggist
American Druggist Merchandising
American Federationist
Automotive Industries
Broadcasting
Business History Review
Business Horizons
Business Week
Chemical Marketing Reporter
Chemical Week
Columbia Journal of World Business

Commerce Today
Conference Board Record
Drug & Cosmetic Industry
Electronic News
Engineering News Record
Factory
Food Processing
Forbes
Forest Industries
Fortune
Fueloil and Oil Heat
Graphic Arts Monthly and the Printing Industry
Harvard Business Review
Industrial Development and Manufacturers Record
Industrial Distribution
Industrial Relations: A Journal of Economy and Society
Industrial Research
Industrial Week
Journal of Business
Law and Policy in International Business
Michigan Business Review
Michigan State University Business Topics
National Petroleum News
Nation's Business
Office
Oil & Gas Journal
Paperboard Packaging
Public Utilities Fortnightly
Research Management
Social Security Bulletin
Survey of Current Business
Textile World
Trusts & Estates
U.S. News & World Report
World Oil

General Business Associations

American Federation of Small Business
American Hotel & Motel Association
National Association of Manufacturers
National Automobile Dealers Association
National Small Business Association

Insurance Periodicals

Best's Review Life/Health Insurance Edition
Best's Review Property/Liability Insurance Edition
Business Insurance
CLU Journal
Insurance
Insurance Journal
Journal of Risk and Insurance
Metropolitan Life Insurance Company Statistical Bulletin
National Underwriter Life & Health Insurance Edition
National Underwriter Property & Casualty Insurance Edition
Spectator

Insurance Associations

American Insurance Association
American Society of Chartered Life Underwriters
Health Insurance Association of America
Institute of Life Insurance
Life Insurance Association of America
National Association of Life Underwriters
Society of Chartered Property and Casualty Underwriters

Management Periodicals

Academy of Management Journal
Administrative Management
Administrative Science Quarterly
Advanced Management Journal
Association Management
California Management Review
Cycles
Hotel and Motel Management
Industrial and Labor Relations Review
Industrial Management
Journal of Purchasing
Journal of the College and University Personnel Association
Manage
Management of Personnel Quarterly
Management Review
*Management Science: Journal of the Institute of Management
      Sciences*

Managerial Planning
Office Supervisors Bulletin
Personnel
Personnel Administration and Public Personnel Review
Personnel Administrator
Personnel Journal
Personnel Management
Personnel Psychology
Production and Inventory Management Journal
Purchasing
SAM Advanced Management Journal
Sloan Management Review
Supervision
Supervisory Management
Training and Development Journal
Training in Business and Industry
Utility Supervision

Management Associations

Administrative Management Society
American Arbitration Association
American Management Association
American Personnel and Guidance Association
American Production and Inventory Control Society
American Records Management Association
American Society for Performance Improvement
American Society for Personnel Administration
American Society for Quality Control
Industrial Management Society
Institute of Management Consultants
International Association Personnel Women
National Management Association
Society for Advancement of Management
Society for Management Information Systems

Marketing Periodicals

Advertising Age
Advertising and Sales Promotion Magazine
Chain Store Age Executives Edition
Distribution Worldwide
Industrial Marketing

Journal of Advertising Research
Journal of Marketing
Journal of Marketing Research
Journal of Retailing
Merchandising Week
Modern Packaging
Progressive Grocer
Public Relations Journal
Sales Management
Stores
Vend

Marketing Associations

American Association of Advertising Agencies
American Marketing Association
Brand Names Foundation
Direct Mail and Marketing Association
National Association of Advertisers
National Association of Retail Merchants

Real Estate Periodicals

Appraisal Journal
Area Development
Construction Review
House & Home
Journal of Property Management
Shopping Center World
Skyscraper Management
World Construction

Real Estate Associations

National Association of Home Builders
National Association of Realtors

Statistics Periodicals

American Statistician
Decision Sciences
Journal of Quality Technology
Operations Research

Statistics Associations

American Statistical Association

Transportation Periodicals

Aviation Week & Space Technology
Defense Transportation Journal
Fleet Owner
Highway User
Pipeline and Gas Journal
Railway Age
Railway Systems Controls
Traffic Digest and Review
Transportation and Distribution Management
Transportation Journal

Transportation Associations

Air Transport Association of America
American Trucking Associations
International Air Transport Association

Appendix B: Constructing the Abstract and Title Page

Two elements of the completed research report that cause problems for many writers are the abstract (sometimes called *epitome, precis,* or *summary*) and the title page. Other prefatory and appended report items, such as Table of Contents, List of Tables, Appendixes, and Bibliography are not included here because such elements are usually set out or described by an adopted style manual.

Writing the Abstract

An abstract is a summary or condensation of a report, thesis, or dissertation that enables a reader to obtain a preview of the report without having to read the entire paper. The abstract may very well be the most important part of a research report, for it is in reading the abstract that the first significant impression of a report is formed in a reader's mind.

An abstract serves three purposes in a research report:

1. It offers a precise summary of the research, which is very important to the busy executive who must evaluate the research importance in a limited time. The abstract is the report in a nutshell.
2. It affords a person the opportunity to keep abreast of developments in a field without reading the complete reports.
3. It provides a convenient means for indexers or catalogers for classifying and filing the report.

Despite its recognized importance, the abstract sometimes does not receive the attention it deserves. Rather, it is sometimes hurriedly constructed as an afterthought by a weary researcher after long periods of writing the report proper.

Because of the abstract's importance, consideration is given here to some general guidelines governing the identification and construction of good abstracts.

Types of Abstracts

Abstracts are usually classified into two general types: the *descriptive abstract* and the *informative abstract.* The descriptive abstract tells only what the report is about, whereas the informative abstract reproduces the most informative factual content of the report.

Descriptive Abstract

The descriptive abstract tells what topics are included in the report, but gives little or no information about what the report says concerning these topics. This type is short and easy to write, but it gives little information. It provides a specialist in the field with enough information about the report to determine whether to read the entire report. The descriptive abstract can contain technical language that will be understood only by the subject-matter group.

A popular form of the descriptive abstract involves the use of three paragraphs. The first paragraph summarizes the introduction section of the report. The middle paragraph summarizes the content or data sections. The last paragraph presents the major conclusions and recommendations.

An offshoot of the descriptive abstract sometimes found is the *review abstract.* The review abstract contains expressions of opinions or judgments about the value or completeness of the report.

The construction of the review abstract appears inconsistent with principles of abstracting; so, probably the best approach here is to use a descriptive-type abstract and furnish a separate section for attached comments, opinions, evaluation, and judgments.

Informative Abstract

The informative abstract states the main points of the report, and it also summarizes the results and conclusions with enough background information to make the results understandable. This type of abstract provides the nontechnical executive with enough knowledge about the report to satisfy most of his administrative needs. The abstract should exclude terms that are not generally understood by the semitechnical people.

The informative abstract is usually more detailed than is the descriptive abstract. The informative abstract should contain:

1. The subject of the report
2. The report purpose or problem
3. Scope
4. Summary of the findings
5. Conclusions
6. Recommendations

The distinction between the two types of abstracts is hazy, and usually abstracts are not exclusively either descriptive or informational. The informative abstract gives everything that is included in the descriptive one; but the inverse is not true. Properly worded, then, the informative abstract can satisfy not only its own purpose, but also that of the descriptive abstract. Thus, it is usually the more desirable type of the two, even though it may be somewhat longer and more general.

Guides for Writing the Abstract

The wealth of information available on writing abstracts includes many rules or guidelines, some of them conflicting. Following are some of the most commonly agreed-upon guidelines which, if followed, will lead to the construction of an effective abstract.

1. *The abstract must be short.* Estimates of a reasonable length range from about three to ten percent of the length of the report itself. This arbitrary definition of the proper length, how-

ever, may be artificially contrived. Although more subjective, a more workable definition may be arrived at in each situation by remembering that if the abstract is too long, it defeats the purpose for which it was written. Conversely, it should not be so short that essential content is left out or accuracy is impaired.

2. *The abstract must be a self-contained unit.* The abstract must stand independent from the report proper because it is very likely that at some time the abstract will be separated from the report and be published or circulated independently. Even if it is not separated from the report, the abstract must be complete in itself if it is to serve its intended purpose. The abstract must not contain, therefore, references to specific sections, pages, charts, or figures included in the report.

3. *The abstract must satisfy reader needs.* The abstract must include enough specific information about the research subject to meet reader requirements. It must contain a statement of the problem and the limitations placed upon it. It must contain the more important results, conclusions, and recommendations. Attention should be given to the presentation of specific information; information that is too general may not be useful.

4. *The abstract must convey the same emphasis as the report.* Ideas contained in the abstract must also appear in the report itself. Ideas that are qualified in the report must also be qualified in the abstract. A person should not be misled nor draw the wrong conclusion from something in the abstract.

5. *The abstract must be objective, precise, and easy to read.* The research report table of contents provides an outline to sections in the report. Construct an abstract rough draft by summarizing each section. Pick up key words, phrases, and sentences. Observe these cautions in writing:
   a. Maintain objectivity; the abstract should be impersonal, unbiased, and noninterpretive.
   b. Exclude guide words such as "Rogers states . . ." or "The author believes. . . ."
   c. Write in prose form; do not shorten by using abbreviations or chopped-sentence construction.

The writing of a good abstract is not easy. An easy-to-read abstract that moves smoothly from one idea to the next, while meeting the conflicting requirements of being both short and detailed, is difficult to obtain. But the good abstract is worth the effort necessary to write it. It is one of the most important parts of the report.

The informative abstract may be presented in an inductive or deductive fashion. The inductive approach presents the report material in the same order as in the original report. The deductive approach, however, leads off with the report's overall conclusion with a subsequent transition to the problem or purpose statement. Scope, methods, and content follow, then, in the same order as presented in the report proper. The deductive approach is recommended here over the inductive (mystery novel) approach.

After the final draft of the abstract is completed and all of the substantive and mechanical criteria are met, it is placed in the report immediately following the title page or preceding the introductory chapter of the report. Either way, it appears among the prefatory material of the report.

Following is a sample abstract written in the deductive style.

ABSTRACT
Roles Portrayed by Women in Print Advertisements, 1987

by Judy Helton

May 1987

The roles women portray in print advertisements are more realistic now than in the past; however, women's roles remain far from being representative of the actual roles women play in today's society. In contrast, men's roles continue to represent accurately the wide variety of roles men play in today's world. These conclusions were drawn from researching the problem: "What is the current status of the roles women portray in print advertisements as compared to the roles men portray." Women's and men's roles were studied in terms of : (1) working roles, (2) nonworking roles, (3) the product advertised and the buying decisions involved, and (4) the interaction of the people shown and their attitudes toward the situations. Over 160 advertisements from the April 1987 issues of eight general-interest publications were studied and analyzed to determine if the mass media's advertisements accurately represent women's roles as they actually exist in American society.

The fact that only 36 percent of the roles portrayed in current advertisements are women's roles indicates that the advertisements do not represent the real world, since over half of the adults in America are women. Working roles portrayed by women in the advertisements analyzed in this study appear to be the least accurate role types in portraying reality. In this study only 18 percent of the people shown as workers were women, and there has been no increase in the roles of women as workers to reflect the substantial addition of women to the labor force since 1982.

More substantial progress has been realized in the nonworking roles in which the more traditional wife and mother roles are being partially replaced to represent more accurately women's roles in society. Nonworking roles of women and men are very similar. These findings, as represented in the advertisements, may reflect a "feeling" in today's society that women and men are indeed equal—except on the job.

The product categories follow traditional associations as women are seen more often than men with only clothing, beauty aids, and office machines. Women are not shown interacting with each other, which may indicate that women are still thought of as dependent upon men in the social system.

Recommended is that further research include a study of the attitudes of: (1) those people that write the advertisements and (2) those people that are exposed to the advertisements—the consumer. This type of research will provide support to the conclusions drawn from the current study of the status of women's roles and will further answer the "why" of this study's findings.

The current 1987 research project's findings recognize both the existence of progress in widening the variety of roles women portray in print advertisements and also the reluctance to change the traditional ways of portraying women. Women's roles are more realistic now than in the past; however, there is still a long way to go before women's roles accurately represent the actual roles women play in today's world.

—Judy P. Helton, Arizona State University

Constructing a Title Page

The title page for a research project is intended to give information and to identify the project. The content of a title page should contain, at the least, these elements: (1) research report title, (2) name and identity of the recipient, (3) name and identity of the author, and (4) place and date.

The title should be as short as possible without becoming vague; it should strike a balance between exactness and brevity. Rarely can a good research report title be shorter than six to ten words, and seldom does one need to be longer than seventeen to twenty words. If a longer title is needed for exactness, then consider using a subtitle to accompany the main title. Especially beware of including wordy or redundant phrases, such as the following:

A report on . . .
An investigation into . . .
An analysis of . . .
A study to determine . . .

Important to include, of course, are the key words under which future researchers would search indexes for the type of information contained in your report. Your report title should be a variation of your research problem statement; so it can carry the idea of what is included and excluded. Since a research report is factual and contains no persuasion, a good title should not be catchy, cute, or structured to attract attention. Neither should the title be in the form of a question; rather, it could imply an *answer* to a question. Pertinent to include are the elements of who, what, why, where, and when.

The title-page entries should be placed on the page in a pleasing manner to reflect a sense of aesthetics. If the title occupies more than one four-inch line, set it out in two or more lines, with each line consisting of logical groupings of words. Arrange these lines in an inverted pyramid format.

Following are two sample title pages, the first for business use and the second for academic use.

EFFECTIVENESS OF THE SALES-TRAINING PROGRAM

FOR CACTUS STATE BANK TELLERS

IN PHOENIX-AREA BRANCHES

Prepared for

Mr. Albert Farmer, Sales Director

Cactus State Bank
411 North Central Avenue
Phoenix, Arizona

Prepared by

George M. Marston

Bank Consultants, Inc.
620 Carlyle Avenue
Los Angeles, California

August 15, 1989

THE FEASIBILITY OF A PROPOSED

WRECKER-TOW SERVICE

IN PHOENIX, ARIZONA

by

Mark K. Peterson

A Research Report

Presented in Partial Fulfillment

of the Requirements for the Course

Business Research Methods

Arizona State University

May 1989

Appendix C: Evaluating the Research Report

The Introductory Section
1. The research problem is:
    a. stated early in the introductory section
    b. analyzed into definite subordinate questions or issues
    c. stated in question form.
2. Hypotheses are unambiguous and stem from the problem statement.
3. The scope of the study is properly distinguished from the study limitations and sets the boundary of the problem.
4. Important or unusual terms are defined, list is discriminate, basis is given, and entries are alphabetized.
5. Assumptions or premises are clear and have been justified by authority, experience, or consequences.
6. No evidence of research findings is given in the introduction.

The Research Design and Methods
of Data Collection

1. The work reflects careful planning, good design, and freedom from deficiencies.
2. The design chosen seems adequate for solving the problem.
3. The proper subjects or sources of information have been used.
4. The sample has been tested for adequacy, or the sample size has been justified.
5. A trial or pilot study has been employed.
6. Reasons for choice of methods are made clear.
7. Questionnaires, tests, interviews, and observations are sound and have been validated.
8. Adequate controls have been provided for all factors that may affect the study.
9. Appropriate statistical methods have been used.
10. The procedures have been carefully stated so any competent investigator could repeat the study and obtain substantially the same results.

Treatment of Data

1. The kinds of data chosen are adequate for solving the problem.
2. Important facts are validated by references to their proof.
3. Data are analyzed both qualitatively and quantitatively; facts are not merely listed.
4. Discussion and interpretation of data are adequate; computations are correct.
5. Negative data are not ignored.
6. Correlation is not mistaken for causation.
7. Irrelevant data are excluded.
8. No bias is evident, conscious or unconscious.
9. Comparisons and contrasts to related studies are included.
10. Comprehensive use is made of current secondary sources, if appropriate.
11. Tables and graphics have been introduced and interpreted.
12. Graphics are technically correct and numbered and captioned; sources are cited; reference subordinated.

The Terminal Section

1. The terminal section has been correctly captioned.
2. If a summary is included, it is distinguishable from the conclusions.

3. The conclusions:
   a. answer the questions or issues raised in the introduction
   b. are stated clearly and concisely; are easily identified as such
   c. are supported by the data presented
   d. are free from mere opinion
4. Any limitations or qualifications of the conclusions are evident and clear.
5. The terminal section contains no new evidence.
6. Implications, applications, and suggestions for further research are judiciously made.

Prefatory and Appended Material

1. The title is descriptive, limited, and correctly worded.
2. The abstract is in deductive style, proportionate, and independent.
3. The prefatory material is properly constructed and sequenced.
4. The table of contents reflects proper organization, classification, and coordination; content entries are clear, descriptive, and grammatically parallel.
5. The appended material is identified and referred to in the text.
6. The bibliography is current and adequate both quantitatively and qualitatively.

The Presentation and Mechanics

1. The report is properly organized and classified and has proper coordination and subordination.
2. Headings or captions are in proper style and are more than mere generalities.
3. Introductory and summary statements or sections have been included.
4. The study is free from unnecessary cross reference.
5. Spelling, grammar, and punctuation are correct.
6. The written presentation is clear and concise.
7. Proper tense has been maintained.
8. Mechanics are consistent with the authorized style manual.
9. Footnotes are complete, in proper form, and accurate.
10. The project is easy to read and understand; it has good word choice and is objective.
11. The entire project reflects care, neatness, and scholarship.

Appendix D: Selecting a Research Problem

The following topic areas may help in selecting a question for a research project. Reviewing the items listed under *Selecting a Problem* in Chapter 2 will help in formulating the research question.

1. The trends and developments in the subject of job stress as reflected in current literature and research.
2. The impact of coupon fraud and misredemption on the manufacturer, the retailer, and the consumer.
3. The effectiveness of current regulations in providing for the financial stability of the commodity trading industry.
4. The nature of strategic planning as is discussed in current literature.
5. Current thought on methods for dealing with employee drug problems.
6. The effect of continuing education upon the career growth of the executive.

7. The impact of "discount" brokers on individual investment in the stock market.
8. The use of arbitrage as a trading tool in the government securities market.
9. The functional contribution of the "floor trader" to the operation of the stock exchanges.
10. Personnel problems presented to the firm because of a language barrier.
11. Problems arising from imposing American work ethics, standards, and customs on foreign employees.
12. Corporate use of short-term negotiable instruments as a cash management tool.
13. The impact of employee benefits as a means of improving employee motivation and productivity.
14. Applications of the cost volume profit analysis concept in small manufacturing companies.
15. The application of the materials management concept in small manufacturing companies.
16. The potential effects of an increase in diesel fuel prices upon the short- and long-range transportation rates and surcharges of agricultural commodities.
17. The effect on retail sales resulting from changes in sales tax.
18. The nature and issues of police performance appraisal.
19. The effect of the physical work environment on the productivity of a data processing center.
20. The breaking point—Identifying the point when progress becomes dysfunctional.
21. Techniques or methods to improve achievement of organization goals through effective use of the data processing resource.
22. Develop a manual for corporate executives concerning effective press relations.
23. Current methods for measuring public response to public relations efforts.
24. The feasibility of implementing a type of express bank teller operation.
25. An application and comparison of the Baumol, Miller-Orr, and Beranek cash management models in bank vault cash control.
26. The effect of product trial through samples on consumer purchase behavior.
27. The effect of the consumer's perception of product positioning on purchase behavior.
28. The costs and benefits associated with the direct deposit of employee's paychecks.

29. The current effects of the legal environment on advertising.
30. Present trends in annual reports to the stockholders and the investing public.
31. The extent, type, and use of sales forecasting methods by small business manufacturers in a selected area.
32. A trend analysis of truck or auto leasing for a designated time period.
33. Guidelines for establishing and administering a contribution policy in a medium-size corporation.
34. Management development practices as reflected in current literature.
35. Problems, issues, and significance of polygraph testing in business.
36. Current practices, problems, and issues in evaluating managers.
37. The current status and trends in control by government legislation of deceptive consumer packaging.
38. An analysis of the computer's impact on the functions of middle management.
39. The role of marketing research in the development and introduction of new products.
40. The development of criteria to formulate a sales training program.
41. A synthesis of current literature on the treatment and cure of drug abuse in business.
42. The risks and benefits of diversification through conglomerate acquisition.
43. Techniques used for evaluating and justifying capital equipment investment projects within manufacturing firms.
44. The concept of "accident proneness" as reflected in the literature from 1919 to present.
45. Methods used in setting standards and evaluating industrial purchasing performance.
46. A synthesis and analysis of thought on the extension of the CPA's attest function to management performance.
47. Characteristics used by company recruiters in evaluating students as prospective employees.
48. Changing court attitudes and their effects regarding legal liability of hospitals.
49. Current attitudes of the relationship of business espionage to market research in business and industry.
50. The role of semiconductor salesmen in collecting and reporting marketing intelligence information.

51. Current sales motivational techniques used in the pharmaceutical industry.
52. Problems, requirements, and solutions involved in the transition from technical specialist to managerial generalist.
53. The effects of group practice upon the supply-demand function of physicians' services.
54. Problems facing commercial banks and their customers in implementing a pre-authorized payment program.
55. Current thought regarding fundamental management problems incurred in international business expansion.
56. The role of management in industrial alcoholism programs.
57. Guidelines for preliminary planning of a management development program.
58. Trends and developments in the rubber industry since 1941.
59. Criteria and techniques for the evaluation of retail store managers.
60. The role of budgets in the planning cycle.
61. A synthesis of current thought on creativity in management.
62. The role of the leisure-time program in industry.
63. Identifying and overcoming barriers to organizational creativity.
64. Management techniques to overcome employee resistance to change.
65. Trends in the administration of the corporate bonus as a motivational device for executives.
66. Current thought on the effects of noise on office workers.
67. The role of sales forecasting in managerial planning.
68. Sensitivity training: The concept and its application to organizational development.
69. The effect of aesthetics on the electric utility industry.
70. Management selection methods of federal agencies as contrasted to private enterprise.
71. Current trends and developments in the printing industry.
72. The effects of imported automobiles on pricing and design in the American automobile industry from 1950.
73. Current thought and legislation on collective bargaining in the public service.
74. The role of black capitalism in the economic development of the urban African-American.
75. Motivation through job enrichment: A synthesis of research.
76. Problems and issues in performance appraisal programs.
77. Problems and issues related to the hiring of the hard-core unemployed.

78. Executive obsolescence: Identification, causes, and correction.
79. The method and extent of disclosure of research and development expenditures as reflected in current literature and company annual reports.
80. Current characteristics of the franchise industry, with implications for the franchisee.
81. Managerial attitudes of local and national industries regarding air-pollution control.
82. Management strategy for dealing with the new-generation manager of the nineties.
83. The feasibility of a shared direct-mail service for small retailers.
84. Current thought regarding sensitivity training in managerial development.
85. Current theory and practice of workers' self-management.
86. Problems, issues, and status of generic versus brand-name drugs.
87. The nature and types of programs used for preretirement counseling by selected firms.
88. Decision analysis—Homeowners selling their own homes.
89. Planning new-product markets for consumer goods.
90. The availability and desirability of handicapped people for business occupations in a selected area.
91. Trends in employment of blacks: 1960 to 1990.
92. An analysis of employment and compensation practices of migrant farm workers.
93. Current thought on group decision making in American corporations.
94. Business opportunities resulting from resolving solid-waste pollution.
95. The effect of repair costs, court procedures, and auto thefts on rising auto insurance rates.
96. The status of sales forecasting as practiced by large manufacturers in a selected area.
97. What personnel directors of selected financial institutions want in a college senior's application letter and resume.
98. The practicality of decision making in security markets using statistical inference.
99. Problems related to entering a franchised business.
100. Trends in published annual reports of electric utilities.
101. Employee performance appraisal in selected manufacturing firms.

102. Relationships between morale, motivation, productivity, and participatory decision making.
103. The response to environmental and social problems of selected industries as reflected in their annual reports.
104. Current thought on the cash bonus as a motivational incentive for executives.
105. Small retail business guidelines for minimizing loss to dishonest employees and shoplifters.
106. Management problems related to research and development in small manufacturing firms.
107. Decision-making factors in the employment interview.
108. Current trends in planning, controlling, and reporting research and development costs for industrial firms.
109. The compatibility of auditing independence and management advisory services: An identification of issues.
110. An appraisal of data security measures with analysis of selected techniques.
111. Drug abuse control in industry: A synthesis of current literature.
112. Executive dismissal policies relative to their effect on the individual.
113. The impact of environmental laws on the electric power industry.
114. Guidelines for implementing a computer security system.
115. The nature and status of the mobile-home industry.
116. Current views and implications of selected barriers to management positions for women.
117. Recruitment and development practices of supporting staff managers in the civil service.
118. The nature and applications of psychographics.
119. Factors considered by electronics manufacturers in choosing foreign assembly facilities.
120. Job design variables related to productivity and satisfaction.
121. The nature of current public relations practices in area hospitals.
122. Trends, developments, and implications of the four-day work week.
123. A synthesis and analysis of current practices in executive development.
124. Current trends in consumerism.
125. The principal controversies affecting legislative reform of private pension plans.
126. Trends in asset investment by private pension funds.

127. The competitive environment of the retail furniture industry.
128. The nature and practicality of the value-added tax.
129. The development and implementation of a book distribution system for a small publishing company.
130. A descriptive analysis of the practical alternatives to the five-day work week.
131. A socio-economic analysis of peak-load pricing of electric rates.
132. Implications of factors contributing to improved safety in air transportation.
133. A descriptive analysis of the current thought on business ethics.
134. The influence of current trends in packaging on consumer buying habits.
135. The practical benefits of the United States space program to the general public.
136. Factors that affect research in the ethical drug industry.
137. Personnel practices and decision making in Japan.
138. The impact of consumerism upon the marketing strategies of business.
139. Sales representative training and development practices in the pharmaceutical industry.
140. The lease-or-buy decision: The nature of leases and decision guidelines.
141. Implications of establishing job enrichment programs in business organizations.
142. The effect of litigation on the accounting profession.
143. Current thought on methods for effective computer systems security.
144. The nature, extent, and implications of hypokinesia in plant and factory workers of selected manufacturing firms.
145. Trends in auditors' legal liability and their implications for current practice.
146. Prevalent trends in work measurement methods for direct labor control.
147. The effects of product liability suits on manufacturing operation.
148. The performance of the established responsibilities of the National Railroad Passenger Corporation (AMTRAK).
149. Trends in the certified public accountant's responsibility for published financial statements.
150. The impact of railroad track abandonment on selected factors.
151. The nature and implications of the environmental conservation movement on the nuclear power industry.

152. The current status of sales forecasting in management.
153. Problems involved in the development of electronic funds transfer systems.
154. Current thought on employees' changing values and their effects on American industry.
155. The current status of discounting by the domestic airlines.
156. Problems and issues in refuse recycling.
157. Factors for reducing risk in potential computer selection.
158. The current status of managerial performance appraisal in business firms.
159. The role of an industrial recreation program for employees in business.
160. Trends and issues in universal product coding.
161. The nature and issues concerning performance appraisal programs.
162. Problems facing women in upper and middle management.
163. Current trends in research and development management practices.
164. Current thought on administering industrial discipline.
165. The status of development and use of geothermal power in the western United States.
166. Trends, developments, and issues in coupon promotion and use.
167. Retirement communities and their economic impact on local governments.
168. Current problems and issues for an advertiser using a sexual advertising theme.
169. The nature of changes in marketing programs due to consumerism.
170. The status of advertising on children's television programs.
171. The implications and adequacy of the objectives of financial reporting.
172. U.S. commercial banking: Profitability of foreign operations.
173. Fraud detection and the independent auditor.
174. An analysis of current thought on mandatory retirement.
175. Trends in the use of management consultants.
176. The nature of selected business forecasting techniques and guidelines for their use.
177. An analysis of the engineered safety systems in the nuclear fuel cycle.
178. Selection and application of an employee appraisal system.
179. Trends in the management of investment portfolios in commercial banks.

180. Potential application of the generic concept of marketing to the delivery of police service.
181. Factors affecting the multi-ethnic organizational compositions of multinational companies.
182. The nature and use of management training and development.
183. Effects and implications of price-level accounting in electric utilities.
184. A comparison of salary increases and job enrichment as motivating factors.
185. The effect of the organizational climate on job satisfaction among hospital nurses.
186. Content of management development programs for women as reflected in current literature.
187. The effectiveness of odd-lot trading as a leading indicator of stock market price trends.
188. The feasibility of applying zero-base budgeting to a school system.
189. The nature of geology in land-use planning and its application to a selected area.
190. Trends and developments in the personal computer market.
191. Trends in the role and the image of the outside salesperson.
192. An analysis of alternative methods of evaluating internal control.
193. Nature and trends in supervising volunteer workers.
194. An examination of the costs and benefits to American business of pollution control regulations.
195. Inventory valuation and decision making with joint products in blood banking.
196. Status and outlook for comparative advertising on U.S. television.
197. Employer attitudes toward hiring the handicapped.
198. Implications of legalized gambling as a source of revenue for state and local governments.
199. The role of business in identifying and dealing with drug use among employees in industry.
200. The potential effects of increased minimum wages on the fast-food industry.
201. A synthesis of pretesting advertising methods.
202. Black-white consumption pattern differences and implications for marketers.
203. Trends and effects of cogeneration as an energy saver in the business community.
204. Issues pertaining to giving local government employees providing essential services the right to strike.

205. The implications of in-plant recycling of polymeric materials.
206. Problems and issues involved in replacement cost accounting.
207. The nature, prevalence, and regulation of deception in advertising.
208. History and current thought on the use and effects of subliminal advertising.
209. The current status of the aquaculture industry in the United States.
210. Business' response to social responsibility: A synthesis of current thought.
211. The nature and implication of the factors affecting small manufacturing business failure.
212. The current status of the health maintenance organization as related to the cost and quality of health care.
213. The nature of occupational stress as reflected in the literature.
214. Trends in coping with employee theft.
215. The status of professional athletes in the advertisement of goods and services.
216. Expectancy theory and its relationship to preentry expectations, job satisfaction, and employee turnover.
217. Human resources information systems: Implications for the personnel manager.
218. Trends in the use of microfilm in information management.
219. The status of strategic planning in business organizations.
220. Trends in compensation for architectural services.
221. A synthesis on the selection, use, and effectiveness of an external consultant.
222. Evolving governmental policies concerning foreign investment in the United States.
223. The effects of institutional constraints on potential industrial applications of cogeneration systems in the United States.
224. The status of psychographic research as related to the selection of advertising media.
225. A synthesis of consumers' brand loyalty for grocery products.
226. Trends in detection and deterrence of computer crime.
227. Performance measurement of scientists and engineers.
228. Impact of computer technology on police services.
229. Implications of selecting engineering managers as top executives for business enterprises.
230. The nature of asset and liability management policy in banking.
231. Effects of marketing strategies within the American brewing industry.

232. The status of regulation of product warranties.
233. Trends in earth integrated architecture.
234. The nature of optimal capital structure planning.
235. Technological obsolescence as a human resource problem.
236. Business response to social accountability in the nineties.
237. The legal and preventative protection afforded foreign consumers from banned or hazardous American-made goods.
238. Effects of import competition on the domestic footwear industry.
239. Factors influencing the demand for and status of women M.B.A. graduates.
240. Current trends in absentee reduction.
241. Vendor rating systems: The current status in high-technology industries.
242. The nature of consumerism and the fundamental consumerism concerns of marketing managers.
243. Reindustrializing America: Correcting America's loss of competitiveness.
244. The nature and current status of dispute resolution mechanisms as an alternative to litigation.
245. Bank security measures: Nature and trends.
246. Implications of personnel turnover in the data processing industry.
247. Guidelines for the purchasing agent in effectively conducting a negotiation session.
248. The nature of strategic planning in the health-care field.
249. The trend and impact of generic products.
250. Current thought on marketing to older consumers.
251. Potential effect of market information on consumer behavior.
252. Privacy considerations of employee personnel files.
253. Nature and status of time management techniques.
254. Managerial application of expectancy theories in modifying employee motivation toward quality of workmanship.
255. The nature and issues of stochastic cost-volume-profit analysis as an approach to decision making.
256. Financial and marketing implications for intercollegiate athletic programs.
257. The implications of time management on executive productivity.
258. Conflict sources and methods of resolution in the business environment.

Index